Dedicated to
My Eternal Companion and Best Friend
Nina
Who first stood with me on Holy Ground

September 2009

i | Forward

Whisperings from
FAR WEST

Forward

They're gone now, the houses, farms, Saints, even the headstones that once marked the martyrs' graves. With the exception of a tranquil temple site, an old Community of Christ chapel, and recently built bookstore, the place that once housed thousands of Latter-day Saints and was the first county seat of Caldwell County, Missouri, is now nothing but empty, serene farmland. However, though the Saints' homes are gone, and the evidence of their once lively existence is scarce, the lives and testimonies of those who lived there can never be forgotten.

In 1984 as my new bride and I visited that lonely place in the middle of some cultivated fields, part of our honeymoon tour of LDS historic sites, the penetrating spirit and sweet peace surrounding that sacred ground at Far West touched our hearts and filled our souls like no other we had visited. It was to us a sort of temple without walls. From that moment, I have felt a deep reverence for, and strong attachment to, that sacred spot of earth which more than a century before was the scene of both holy events and severe persecutions.

The memories of the significant revelations that the Far West Saints received there, the spiritual manifestations they enjoyed, and the supreme courage under fire they displayed are not forgotten. The Abrahamic trials which those faithful Saints passed through, and which in turn sanctified that holy ground, continue to speak from the past to any and all who have ears to hear, with such a force as to guarantee that their legacy will remain.

The historically based poems, hymns, ballads, and other prose contained within these pages, are written with the express purpose of giving voice to those Saints whose lives and experiences make sacred, what the Lord himself declared to be holy ground. May all who read the sentiments expressed within these pages not only increase in their knowledge of the fascinating history of Far West, but may they feel the power of the testimony and admire the unshakable faith of those whose sanctifying sacrifices provide the real meaning and sentiments behind these; *"Whisperings from Far West."*

Contents

Chapter One	The Beginnings
Chapter Two	Jonah's Gourd
Chapter Three	Holy Ground
Chapter Four	The House of God
Chapter Five	Refiner's Fire
Chapter Six	The Danites
Chapter Seven	The Church's Political Motto
Chapter Eight	Revelations at Far West
Chapter Nine	Adam Ondi Ahman
Chapter Ten	Blessing of the Children
Chapter Eleven	The Elder's Journal (Far West Edition)
Chapter Twelve	Growth of Persecution
Chapter Thirteen	Kirtland Camp
Chapter Fourteen	War Upon the Saints
Chapter Fifteen	David W. Patten: Apostle & Martyr
Chapter Sixteen	Siege of Far West
Chapter Seventeen	Covenant Committee
Chapter Eighteen	Death of a City

Chapter Nineteen	Still There
Appendix A	Limericks of Life in Far West
Appendix B	Revocation of Extermination Order

Chapter One

The Beginning

It was September 1836, when the activities that eventually led to the foundation and growth of Far West actually began. The Saints' focus on, and attempts at establishing, Zion in Jackson County, Missouri had been thwarted by mobocracy and bigotry. The suffering Saints who had been driven from their homes in Jackson County, and many also from Clay County, had moved into the outskirts of Ray County.

Additionally, Zion's Camp had recently concluded its march and was disbanded when its purpose was declared by God to be something other than that which many of the Saints had hoped and waited for, an armed retaking of their lands. The Lord had also spoken to these suffering Saints through their Prophet, Joseph Smith Jr., and had chastised them for their weakness, though it is also true that He promised them that their dream of Zion was not completely dead, merely postponed for a season. Thus, the Saints clung to that hope, that dream, of Zion's future redemption.

That the majority of the Saints truly longed for and expected such a redemption is evidenced by the charges those Saints leveled against a few of their Church leaders who, rather than wait for that redemption of Zion, actually sold their lands in Jackson County. That act was almost incomprehensible in the minds of the Zion focused Saints and motivated them to seek an accounting from those leaders.[1]

Given those powerful desires for the redemption and establishment of Zion, which dwelt in the hearts of the vast majority of the Missouri Saints, these words of the Lord, as revealed in the Doctrine and Covenants, must have both stung, and yet in a way also encouraged, the displaced and anxious Saints, who were looking south and yearning for Zion:

> Behold, I say unto you, were it not for the transgressions of my people, speaking concerning the Church and not individuals, they might have been redeemed even now. But behold, they have not learned to be obedient to the things which I required at their hands, but are full of all manner of evil, and do not impart of their substance, as becometh saints, to the poor and afflicted among them; And are not united according to the union required by the law of the celestial kingdom; And Zion cannot be built up unless it is by the principles of the law of the celestial kingdom; otherwise I cannot receive her unto myself. And my people must needs be chastened until they learn obedience, if it must needs be, by the things which they suffer....Therefore… it is expedient in me that mine elders should wait for a little season, for the redemption of Zion.[2]

It was with those powerful words of their God still ringing in their minds and hearts that so many of the Saints had gathered near Shoal Creek, in Northwest Missouri.[3] One can almost feel the anxiousness which motivated them to stay close to the borders of their beloved Zion. Understanding their desire and its roots, makes it easy to understand their undying hopes for a brighter future, their commitment to repent, reorganize, and to grow strong so that they might thereafter return "in a little season"[4] and redeem the Zion of their God.

It must have been for them like the children of Israel, looking into Canaan, whose spies had declared their promised land to be beautiful beyond measure, but similarly unconquerable. For that reason, the Missouri Saints gathered for a time in what was to become Caldwell County, anxiously looking back toward the Zion they loved and waiting for the glorious day when as their God had promised, it would be redeemed. It is essential to understand, and to feel what was in the hearts of those Saints, in order to then understand how it was that Far West could grow so quickly, and why it was they clung so desperately to the holy ground, that was to be their Zion.

Waiting for Zion

A Parable

There sat upon the grassy knoll, swept by September's winds, a man with a weathered face, whose intense blue eyes gazed, fixed and determined, southward, down a long well rutted wagon trail. His worn clothing, his demeanor and the soil stained powerful hands, bespoke that he was a farmer. He seemed not to blink or flinch, but appeared to focus on the wisps of smoke arising on the horizon far to the south. The lines of dirt upon his cheeks, left by tears which once had flowed freely, seemed to stand out on his reddened jaws. His breathing was labored, his shoulders sloped, yet still he seemed to radiate strength. Behind him were three mounds, one large and two small, of freshly spaded earth which revealed the tragic labor his soil covered hands had just completed.

Suddenly from the south there rode swiftly on the back of a large sweat soaked steed, a rough looking man, pistol strapped to his side, musket laying across his lap, blood lust showing clearly in his eyes. He rode with a purpose, straight toward the weary man, who, though he saw the rider approaching, still did not move. As the rider drew near, he reigned in his mighty steed and looked down disapprovingly upon the farmer, who seemed so small in the shadow of the horse and rider, and then laughed. The sound was loud, the feeling behind it cruel, the mocking intention clear, yet still the farmer gazed south. Aggravated by the lack of any response to his presence, his laugh, or his pretense of awesome power, the rider looked intently at the farmer and spoke:

You've lost you fool, your life's a waste
Your wife and kids are dead
There is no Zion, never was
Your people have all fled

The prophecies were clearly lies
Your prophet but a fake

*Your Zion never will appear
Give up, your life's at stake*

The words hung heavily about the weary, still sitting, farmer, whose eyes never-the-less remained fixed to the south. Without looking at his challenger, and with a powerful resolve that seemed impossible could come from such a weary looking creature, the farmer spoke from the shadow of the mobocrat:

*It's Zion that I'm waiting for
I know that it shall come
Where with my family and my God
At last I'll be at home*

With another derisive chuckle, the horseman turned and rode away, his heavy laughter filled the air, lingering long after the horse and rider were out of sight.

II

Soon, slowly marching up the rutted road, with saber at his side, and musket slung over his shoulder, there came a soldier. His bearing revealed his training and discipline, his uniform bespoke his command: The Army of America. His three-cornered hat seemed strangely out of place, a reminder of the brave soldiers who, under President Washington, had survived the cold at Valley Forge, and who fought to victory in New Jersey. As he approached the knoll and the gazing man, he paused and sighed. His look was one of compassion, even shame, as if he wished he could help the solitary farmer; as if he wished he did not have to say what was on his heart. Yet the soldier knew he had to speak, and so at last, with some tenderness in his voice, he said:

*Give up my friend, you cannot win
Your Nation's turned away
And politicians rule your land
Give up and flee away*

*Militias governed by the weak
Have made your people cower
The states are free to cast aside
Our Constitution's power*

*I am but one, and cannot stop
The mobs who steal your land
Your cause is just, but I am weak
And will not take a stand*

Then tears began to flow from the soldier's eyes as he mumbled these final words to the farmer:

*It shames me, that you're suffering so
On lands I bought with blood
The liberty we fought to give
Destroyed by hatred's flood*

*But since I'm weak and cannot help
Your Zion will not be
You must forget, give up that hope
Seek not, lost liberty*

This time the solemn farmer, chanced a glance toward the now trembling soldier, as their eyes met, they both understood at once, and for just a moment the soldier's grief filled face, changed to reflect a wry smile, then he heard the old man speak:

*It's Zion that I'm waiting for
I know that it shall come
Where with my family and my God
At last I'll be at home*

III

As the soldier marched on, the old man's gaze returned to the south and the smile faded from his face. It was not long until he spied a wagon, richly loaded with dry goods, food stuffs, farming implements, and fine furniture. The driver was a heavy-set man, with a plump and jovial face, who, as he drew near, reined his wagon to a halt. A look of concern spread across his face as he surveyed the fresh mounds of earth behind the farmer, but that was quickly replaced by a sort of greedy benevolence that appeared on his face, as one who realized there was a profit to be made. After looking over the scene once more he fixed his eyes on the old farmer and spoke:

I see my friend, your goods are lost
And poverty's your end
Your faith in Zion, left you broke
But I'll still be your friend

Forget that dream whose time is past
And sell your land to me
Thus turn your poverty to wealth
Let money set you free

Though continuing to look toward the south, the old man slowly raised his soiled hand to his chest and felt the deed to his land in Jackson County which he still carried with him, safely tucked into an inner pocket. He then carefully looked over the loaded wagon, filled to overflowing with the goods of the world, then looked carefully behind him to the fresh mounds of earth. He paused, then at length turned to look south again, speaking as he did with renewed vigor:

It's Zion that I'm waiting for
I know that it shall come
Where with my family and my God
At last I'll be at home

The wagon master shrugged and chuckled to himself, then moved on, thinking in his soul how thankful he was for the security and peace he felt sitting among his load of goods. He then thought to himself; "Soul, thou hast laid up much goods for these many years, take thine ease, eat, drink and be merry,"[5] then on he moved, not giving the farmer a second thought.

IV

It was not long before there appeared on the road, one whom the old farmer knew very well. Even from a distance, the sight of his old friend approaching, caused a flood of memories to well up within his heart. He remembered their missionary service together, the sweet communion with the Holy Spirit they had both enjoyed as they sat at the feet of the Prophet Joseph and heard him speak of Zion, the faith with which they had left their eastern lands and homes to move to Jackson County, and there prepare for the promised glories to come. As the traveler approached him, head hung down, he walked as one with a terrible burden, but as he saw his old friend seated on the knoll and staring south from whence he himself had just come, he picked up his pace and leaving the road, ascended the knoll to sit beside his old friend. For the longest time he simply sat there and though neither of them spoke, they both softly wept for the cause of Zion. At long last the traveler looked to his dear friend and spoke with questioning eyes:

'Tis gone my friend, our Zion, our hopes
I cannot understand
What happened to our Prophet's dream?
Where went our promised land?

I once believed in Zion's call
And lived to see it grow
But now my faith has fled, dear friend
I know not where to go

Should we forget, return to lives
We lived before we knew
Of Joseph's teachings, God's great gifts
I once was sure were true?

Why sit you here, can you believe
In spite of all we've lost
Why do you look on blessings gone?
How do you count the cost?

The old and humble farmer sighed deeply, looking to the ground as if searching for the right words to say, the right way to convey the spirit in his heart. He then fixed his gaze upon his friend and with love, emboldened by the power of the Holy Spirit which still radiated from his eyes, he humbly spoke:

It's Zion that I'm waiting for
I know that it shall come
Where with my family and my God
At last I'll be at home

After what seemed like ages, the traveler smiled, shook the soil stained hand of his friend, slowly rose, and proceeded to another knoll where he sat, and then fixed his own gaze toward the south, to await the redemption of his beloved Zion.

V

It was late afternoon, when the last traveler appeared on the muddy and trenched road. He walked with a purpose, the demeanor of one who knew where he was headed and what he must do once he got there. As the traveler approached, the old man shifted his gaze and fixed it upon the approaching, well known man. Immediately he felt his heart begin to race, and his fear to increase, for he dreaded this confrontation that he knew must come. It was not long before the traveler arrived and stood before the old farmer. As he looked down, the famer stood, and they stared into each other's eyes. The traveler was the express image of the farmer, and the old man knew that he was at last, confronting himself. Without any discernable emotion, the newly arrived image of himself spoke:

Levi, we've sat here far too long
It's time we moved along
Our family's now in our God's hands
To give up can't be wrong

We've done our best, we've sought the dream
Obeyed our prophet's voice
Our God cannot expect much more

He's given us the choice

Look not for Zion, we have failed
To live celestially
It's simply far beyond our power
Give up and come with me

The weary, yet firm, farmer looked deeper into his own soul, smiled at himself, then sat back down and almost shouted:

It's Zion that I'm waiting for
I know that it shall come
Where with my family and my God
At last I'll be at home

By the end of his words the image of himself had faded and the farmer felt welling within him a renewed hope.

VI

As evening set upon the knoll, the farmer's eyes began to close, and he soon lowered his head in sleep. The September night was cold, but the farmer was beyond its biting cold grasp. In fact, he began to feel a great warmth, which filled his soul while also warming him from outside. He could tell through his eyelids that he was suddenly surrounded by a brilliant light and marveled that dawn had come so soon. As he opened his eyes, he saw standing before him, one who he immediately knew to be his Lord. He fell to his knees and began to weep, wanting to touch the Savior, but being painfully aware of his soiled and weathered hands, and unkempt appearance. His anxiety at how he looked, and his bright recollections of his many weaknesses began to build a powerful fear within him, until the brilliant being spoke and called him by name:

Arise Levi, and come to me
Your journey now is through
The Zion you have long since sought
Has finally come to you

With that the old farmer rose to his feet and wiped his eyes. As he walked toward his Savior, the Lord turned slightly to reveal standing behind him the old man's wife and two daughters. Thrilled to his core, the old farmer ran to his loved ones and embraced and kissed them, then turned back to his Lord, fell to the ground and wet his feet with tears of gratitude. In the end, as the Lord, the farmer and his family walked away from the knoll, the old man looked back to where he had long sat and where he had faced down the many travelers. With a smile on his face and a feeling of gratitude in his heart, he beheld there a fourth mound of earth with a wooden grave marker on which was written these words:

It's Zion that I'm waiting for
I know that it shall come
Where with my family and my God
At last I'll be at home

Chapter Two

Jonah's Gourd

As the number of the Latter-day Saints gathering along the Shoal Creek in Northwest Missouri increased, the foundations of what was to become the city of Far West were already being laid. Homes, businesses, even a post office began to spring up. This rapidity of the influx of the Saints to the area of Far West led the Prophet Joseph Smith to remark in his journal:

> The Saints having gathered in considerable numbers on Shoal Creek, Missouri petitioned for an act of incorporation for a new county, which was granted about the middle of December, under the name of Caldwell County, from which time a fresh impetus was given to the gathering, *and the county grew like Jonah's gourd.*[6]

In the context of the times it seems that the prophet was simply alluding to the well-known Old Testament scripture, applying the portion about the rise of the gourd, to the swift rise of the Mormon community in Far West, a land which not long before was just wilderness. However, with the hindsight of history we can see that this short but powerful metaphor was not only an apt description of what had happened, but was also a precise, prophetic declaration of future Far West events.

Joseph's meaning in his reference to the gourd of Jonah should be familiar to most who have read the story as it appears in the Old Testament. While there are many aspects to Jonah's tale, which in total expound upon the tender mercies of God, most people, especially those with only a basic familiarity with the Bible, will focus upon the part of the story where the reluctant Jonah is swallowed by a whale or a great fish. However, read in context, and under the influence of the spirit, a deeper analysis of Jonah's story reveals that all the chapters leading up to the final chapter, including the story of Jonah in the fish's belly, were merely background. They form a sort of running foundation for the powerful lesson that God teaches Jonah, and all who read his story, through the medium of the gourd.

As Jonah's final chapter unfolds, we see him sitting on a hill outside of what had been an extremely wicked Nineveh, suffering in the heat of the sun and waiting to see if the Lord would destroy the city as he had prophesied. As Jonah sat there, the Lord caused a gourd to grow up out of the ground which provided comforting shade for his head. It seems clear that Joseph Smith, in his allusion to the growth of Far West as Jonah's gourd, recognized that it was indeed a miracle that the gourd would grow to such size and stature as to provide such relief to Jonah, in so short a span of time.

Therein is found one powerful symbol in the fact that the rapid growth of the gourd provided comfort to a suffering Jonah, similar to the rapid rise of Far West, which in turn provided refuge and comfort to the suffering Saints who had fled Jackson and Clay counties. Both city and gourd provided a respite, granted by a merciful God to his suffering children. More interesting however, is the truth that as the writings in this book and other recorded histories testify, the Far West period was merely a momentary respite, for as with Jonah's gourd, the city of Far West was not to last.

The scripture goes on to record that in order to teach His prophet a lesson of mercy and compassion, and to also provide a sort of eternal perspective, the Lord sent a worm that destroyed the gourd almost as quickly as it had grown up, until as the scriptures record: "it smote the gourd that it withered"[7] again exposing Jonah to the suffering he had experienced before. Jonah was angry for the loss of the soothing relief which the gourd had provided, and the Lord used that anger to teach him. Jonah's lesson included the knowledge that the Lord loves the individual, and provides relief in their times of sore tribulations, yet another aspect of that lesson was that the Lord will also have a tried and chastened people.[8]

Both of those lessons were applicable to the Saints of Far West, and were lessons that would no doubt travel with them to Nauvoo, Winter Quarters, and at last, the Salt Lake Valley and beyond!

On a deeper level, it should be noted that it was Jonah's actions that led him into his suffering; suffering that was required to teach him the lessons he seemingly wouldn't learn otherwise. So it was with the Saints who in part had failed to heed the Lord's counsel given to them in Jackson County, and so by their actions were brought to suffer. In fact, it is significant to note that it was at Far West where the Prophet Joseph, in response to news from the nearby settlement of Hawn's Mill about the massacre of some of its inhabitants, remarked: *"Up to this day God had given me wisdom to save the people who took counsel. None had ever been killed who [had abided] by my counsel"*[9] It was the failure to heed the Lord's counsel that led Jonah to his difficulties, just as it was the failures of the Jackson County Saints that had led to their expulsion from that county and flight to the area of Far West.

As a part of His final lesson to Jonah the Lord significantly refers to the gourd describing its progress with this language: "Thou hast had pity on the gourd, for which thou hast not labored, neither madest it grow, *which came up in a night, and perished in a night"*[10]

Therein lays the powerful prophetic description of what was to become of Far West. For of all the Church history sites, there is none that better fits the description of a city, which rose to great prominence and then totally perished in so short a span. Visitors to Far West in this century will find nothing of its homes, businesses, streets, even the cemetery has been lost. All that remains is the holy spot of ground where the temple cornerstones were laid. It is not difficult today for one standing on the temple lot and surveying the outlying fields (while simultaneously pondering the descriptions of the city of Far West as it once appeared) to see in Joseph's simple comment about Jonah's gourd, a prophetic vision for the rise and fall of the city and people of Far West.

<u>Jonah's Gourd</u>

They rose in a night
      Both city and gourd
Yea, both came about
      By will of the Lord

Each brought sweet refuge
      To suffering Saints
Each showed that our God
      Doth hear our complaints

They died in a night
      A refuge no more
But lessons they taught
      Remain evermore

Chapter Three

Holy Ground

In all of holy writ there are but three places that the Lord specifically describes as, or declares to be, holy ground. It is significant that of those three areas, two are in the Middle East and one is in the Midwestern United States, the latter being the land of Far West. The fact that the spot of earth comprising Far West was so supremely special seemed to be intuitively and spiritually understood by many in Far West, even before the Lord declared it to be so.

Early on in the settlement of the Far West area, William W. Phelps, who was at the time a member of the branch presidency, wrote a letter dated July 7, 1837 from Far West to the leading brethren in Kirtland, Ohio, giving them a glowing report about the progress of the Saints in Far West. At the conclusion of his letter he makes this interesting observation: "If the brethren abroad are wise, and will come on with means, and help enter the land and populate the county and build the Lord's house, *we shall soon have one of the most precious spots on the globe...*[11]

On the 4th of September of that same year the Prophet Joseph Smith wrote an encouraging and spirit filled letter to John Corrill who was then serving as a clerk for the High Council, an agent to the Church and the keeper of the Lord's storehouse at Far West. His letter was also generally directed to those Joseph designated as the "whole Church in Zion." The Prophet Joseph began his letter with praises to God for the many blessings He had bestowed upon the Saints, then interestingly refers to God's deliverance of those Saints from the hands of their enemies and the "*planting*" of the Saints in what he called a "*Heavenly or Holy place.*"[12]

Less than eight months later, April 26, 1838, the Prophet Joseph who was then residing at Far West, received a revelation from God which was later to become Section 115 of the Doctrine and Covenants. While that section is rich with various revelations which will be covered in a later chapter, for the purposes of this chapter, it is only significant to note verse 7, wherein the Lord proclaims: "Let the city, Far West, be a holy and consecrated land unto me; and it shall be called most holy, *for the ground upon which thou standest is holy.*"[13]

Thus, the earlier views of both W.W. Phelps and Joseph Smith, referring to Far West as a special or holy place, were later affirmed by the Lord through that sweet revelation concerning the land of Far West. Additionally, that truth will also be affirmed to those in our day who visit that now quiet and lonely spot of ground in West Central Caldwell County and hear the spirit testify that it truly is a sanctified and holy spot of earth, in other words, holy ground.

Holy Ground

On Sinai's great and fiery height

    Where Moses turned to see the sight

        And Great I AM spoke words of light

            That spot was Holy Ground (Exodus 3:5)

Where Jericho guarded Canaan's fount

    And Joshua sought to take account

        There the Lord's Captain, from the mount

            Declared it Holy Ground (Joshua 5:15)

Where prairie grass was wet with dew

    Sweet Zion filled the prophet's view

        And Far West from the wilds grew

            There too, was Holy Ground (D & C 115:7)

Chapter Four

The House of God

From the days of Kirtland, the Saints became a temple loving, temple building people, and it was no different for the Saints who were now rapidly growing in numbers in Far West. The original plan for the Mormon development of Jackson County, had included plans for several temples, and it is not strange that those Saints, who had been recently expelled, would still so strongly desire to build a temple. Interestingly, today the only landmark remaining of the once vibrant Mormon colony of Far West is the temple lot. That site was the scene of many spiritual and prophetic occurrences making up an important part of the history of Far West and the Church, and that spot has remained a sacred and holy place in the century and a half since the city's demise.

The Far West temple site was originally selected by Presidents W.W. Phelps and John Whitmer, but there arose some question as to the right of the Presidency at Far West to appoint or select the place for the building of the Lord's house. In fact in a meeting of the High Council, held on April 3,1837 at Far West, the high councilors voted to require the presidency to give an explanation to a list of several questions or grievances, the first and second being; "*First-by what authority was this place [Far West] pointed out as a city and [a place for a] house of the Lord and by whom? Second-by what authority was a committee appointed and ordained to superintend the building of the House of the Lord?*"[14] The answers to those interrogatories from the High Council are not recorded, but they must have been satisfactory since the Saints at Far West proceeded to lay the ground work for the building of the temple.

On July 3, 1837, there were already over fifteen hundred Saints in the Far West area, most of whom had gathered together on that day to lay the foundations of what they believed would be the second temple to be constructed in their dispensation, since the temples planned for Jackson County seemed at the time, to be beyond their power to build. In a letter to the brethren in Kirtland,

W.W. Phelps described the touching scene that he witnessed as the Saints prepared the Far West temple site on that significant summer day:

> "*Monday, the 3rd of July, was a great and glorious day in Far West more than fifteen hundred Saints assembled at this place and half-past-eight in the morning, after prayer, singing and an address, they proceeded to break the ground for the Lord's House. The day was beautiful; the spirit of the Lord was with us. An excavation for this great edifice, one hundred and ten feet long by eighty feet broad was nearly finished...*"[15]

Interestingly, there is no record of any significant progress on the temple site after that day, and in August of 1837, the High Council in Far West voted to "go on moderately and build a house unto the name of the Lord in Far West"[16] They determined that they would proceed as they had means, and Edward Partridge was appointed as treasurer for that purpose, with Isaac Morley as his assistant. The question on whether they should be pushing for a temple and hesitancy to begin with the actual construction, were no doubt based in part upon the promptings of the Holy Spirit. For at the latter end of October, after the Prophet Joseph Smith had arrived at Far West and begun to regulate the affairs of the Church in that area, among the corrective decisions he made was the decision that they should wait upon the Lord with regard to building the temple. The prophet recorded: "*Also voted...that the building of the House of the Lord be postponed until the Lord shall reveal it to be his will to have it commenced.*"[17]

With that decision the work of preparing to build a temple at Far West stopped and remained dormant for the next five months. Then on April 26,1838, while at Far West, the Prophet Joseph received a revelation from the Lord concerning both the City of Far West and the building of the Lord's temple there. Said the Lord:

> *Therefore, I command you to build a house unto me, for the gathering together of my saints, that they may worship me. And let there be a beginning of this work,*

> *and a foundation, and a preparatory work, this following summer; And let the beginning be made on the fourth day of July next; and from that time forth let my people labor diligently to build a house unto my name; And in one year from this day let them re-commence laying the foundation of my house. Thus let them from that time forth labor diligently until it shall be finished, from the corner stone thereof unto the top thereof, until there shall not anything remain that is not finished. Verily I say unto you, let not my servant Joseph, neither my servant Sidney, neither my servant Hyrum, get in debt any more for the building of a house unto my name; But let a house be built unto my name according to the pattern which I will show unto them. And if my people build it not according to the pattern which I shall show unto their presidency, I will not accept it at their hands. But if my people do build it according to the pattern which I shall show unto their presidency, even my servant Joseph and his counselors, then I will accept it at the hands of my people.* [18]

Pursuant to this revelation from God, on July 4, 1838, at what can only be described as the pinnacle of activity in Far West, there was a sacred and holy convocation in which the cornerstones of the Lord's House were officially laid. The Prophet Joseph describes that exciting event:

> *The order of the day was splendid. The procession commenced forming at 10 o'clock a.m. in the following order: First, the infantry (militia); second, the patriarchs of the Church; the president, vice president, and orator; the Twelve Apostles, presidents of the stakes, and High Council; Bishop and counselors; architects, ladies and gentlemen. The Calvary brought up the rear of the large procession, which marched to music and formed a circle, with the ladies in front, round the excavation. The southeast cornerstone of the Lord's House in Far West, Missouri, was then laid by the presidents of the stake, assisted by twelve men. The southwest corner by the presidents of the Elders, assisted by twelve men. The*

northwest corner by the Bishop, assisted by twelve men. northeast corner by the president of the Teachers, assisted by twelve men. This house is to be one hundred and ten feet long, and eighty feet broad. The oration was given by President Rigdon, at the close of which was a shout of Hosanna, and a song composed for the occasion by Levi W. Hancock, was sung by Solomon Hancock. The most perfect order prevailed throughout the day.[19]

Sadly, the tragedies and persecution that were soon to befall the Saints would defeat the express purpose of that perfect day. The actions of the mob through the following months prevented the Saints from building the House of the Lord at Far West. In spite of that fact, it is important to note that the cornerstones laid in place that day, were, at least in part, subsequently re-laid in a sacred, quiet meeting the following April. The events of that later, small, apostolic gathering and placement of the cornerstones, fill many with a sincere hope, prayer, and faith that one day, there will be at that very site in Far West, a house of God built unto the Lord's name.

Built Unto His Name

*Desiring a place among His Saints
Where God could come, His truths make known
Among Israel, Jehovah sought
A tabernacle, earthly throne*

*In Canaan, Israel's promised land
Through Samuel, word to David came
From Solomon the Lord would seek
A house built to His Holy name*

*On promised land, Nephi did strive
To build a house unto his Lord
Like Solomon's most precious place
Where Saints could go, to hear God's word*

Through time, God's children oft would move
To find peace in, a sacred place
There too God sought a holy house
From which to teach of heavenly grace

II

Driven, expelled from Jackson's land
Then finding rest on Holy Ground
The Far West Saints', did yearn to build
A house where God's truths would abound

Like David, yearning filled their souls
Desire drove them to proceed
Their hopes were pure, their faith was strong
Reflecting deep, eternal need

Yet Far West Saints were told to wait
Righteous desires to God must yield
'Twas He, who must command the work
Before they sought His house to build

III

Sweet spring, the words from Heaven came
Revealed to Joseph's humble heart
"Go build a house unto my name"
"Require each Saint to do their part"

July fourth dawned and Saints rejoiced
As cornerstones were laid with prayer
Beginning of God's Far West home
Hosannas filled the prairie air

IV

Yet, angry mobs expelled the Saints
Thus never did their temple stand
Though twelve returned one sacred morn
Fulfilling God's holy command

Foundation stone they rolled in place
At southeast corner, there to stay
Expressing hopes to one day build
When God would open up the way

That cornerstone, unmoved, still waits
And has since those apostles came
That day when Far West Saints shall see
A house built to God's holy name

Chapter Five

The Refiner's Fire

Not long after that sacred dedication day the persecutions against the Saints at Far West and throughout Missouri intensified in the extreme. No doubt, the sweet and powerful commitment expressed by the Saints in seeking a house of God, had aggravated the adversary, who then seemed to inspire and stir up the mobs with exceptional speed. The trials the Saints were to face thereafter were not just from the persecutions of outsiders. Many within the Church caved in to pressures or temptations from the evil one, then turned and persecuted those who had been their fellow Saints. However, many others stayed faithful and were conversely sanctified, purified, and even made stronger by all that they suffered.

In speaking of why the Saints had suffered in their past attempts to establish a Zion society the Lord had said:

> "I, the Lord, have suffered the affliction to come upon them, wherewith they have been afflicted, in consequence of their transgressions ...Behold, I say unto you, there were jarrings, and contentions, and envyings, and strifes, and lustful and covetous desires among them; therefore by these things they polluted their inheritances."[20]

Sadly, the events and activities in and around Far West, demonstrate that some of the Saints still had not learned that lesson from Jackson County. That is not to say that their struggles with living the celestial law in any way justified the terrible atrocities that were heaped upon them by their vile persecutors. However, the concept of consecration lies at the heart of why it is that some of the Far West Saints endured with faith and patience, even through the terrible ordeal of their expulsion, while others chose to be offended and turned away from their faith, in some cases even joining the enemies of the Church.

It was during these trying and difficult times at Far West that many of the important and well-known leaders of the Church were excommunicated or cut off from among the Saints. Thus, in that significant and regrettable way, Far West revealed itself to be a sort of crucible, the oven in which the refiner's fire burned so very hot.

Throughout the growth of the Church at Far West the impact of the refiner's fire was revealed to us in numerous councils where charges and countercharges were made, and pride seemed rampant among many of the Saints. Their small Missouri community, appointed by God as a gathering place, reflected scenes similar to those in the Nephite Church just prior to the Savior's appearance wherein; *"Some were lifted up in pride, and others were exceedingly humble; some did return railing for railing, while others would receive railing and persecution and all manner of afflictions, and would not turn and revile again, but were humble and penitent before God."*[21] So it was for the Saints at Far West.

The proud and unrepentant were identified and cut off, while the humble endured great pains, yet remained faithful. Thankfully in some cases, those who were cut off followed the example of the prodigal son and after coming to themselves in later years, they returned to the Church. Nothing written here should be taken as a final judgment upon their actions. Few, if any, of the Saints of our day could ever identify with the struggles and challenges that the Far West Saints endured.

However, a review of the paths that some of the Church's leaders took resulting from the Far West period is instructive to the Saints in our day in three ways. First, it demonstrates the truth behind the proverb which declares that *"Pride goeth before destruction and an haughty spirit before a fall."*[22] Second, it helps us to see that it is possible for those who have lost their way from the fold, and even turned to persecute the Church, to return. Third, the life stories captured in these sonnets that follow, reveal that even through the greatest tests and trials, some can endure well and remain faithful. The circumstances behind the apostasy of some and endurance of others, among the leaders at Far West is important to the Saints of our day, as we near the time of the coming of our Lord, and the refining persecutions that must attend thereto. May we all learn from them.

Leaders at Far West

The Sonnets

Lyman Wight

Brother Lyman Wight was baptized by Oliver Cowdery in 1830, and was soon thereafter made a high priest in the restored gospel. He served a successful mission for the Church in Ohio and moved with many Saints to Jackson County to establish Zion. During the conflict in Jackson County, Lyman was one of the brethren who traveled to Kirtland to tell the Prophet Joseph of their troubles, and it was his plea to the Prophet which in turn led to the formation of Zion's Camp. Lyman not only recruited Saints to go with the camp but went himself and remained faithful through their trials. After Zion's Camp was disbanded Lyman remained in Missouri and eventually settled at Adam-Ondi-Ahman, north of Far West.[23]

Sadly, on April 24, 1837 at Far West, the apostle Elder David W. Patten, preferred a charge against Lyman Wight for "teaching erroneous doctrines"[24] The summary of what he had taught was that the Church as a body "...were under a telestial law, because God does not whip under the celestial law, therefore He took us out of doors to whip us, as a parent took his children out of doors to chastise them, and that the book of Doctrine and Covenants was a telestial law..."[25] In response to the charges Lyman was required by the Presidency at Far West, consisting of W.W. Phelps and John Whitmer, as well as by the High Council, to make an acknowledgement to the council and the churches where he had taught that doctrine, that he was in error.

The record is silent as to Lyman's response to that requirement, though it is interesting to note that he appears later as one of the accusers of W.W. Phelps and John Whitmer on the charge against them for selling lands in Jackson County. Whatever, Lyman's view and actions taken in response to the chastisement, he stayed faithful to the Church throughout the difficulties at Far West. By May of 1838 he was acknowledged as a Colonel in the militia and had charge of protecting the Saints in Adam-Ondi-Ahman, or as the Saints nick named it, "Diahman". Later in an effort to appease the mobs and thus protect the Saints, Lyman along with the Prophet Joseph Smith, volunteered to surrender himself up to false charges and to be tried by the mob controlled legal system. Near the end of the Saints' sojourn in Far West, Lyman was captured and imprisoned with the Prophet Joseph by the treachery that occurred there.

Lyman continued to serve the Church, and was later ordained an apostle and named the "Wild Ram of the Mountain." However, with the death of the Prophet Joseph he seemed to lose his bearings. He had, prior to Joseph's death, obtained permission from Joseph to lead some of the Saints who had been lumbering wood in Wisconsin for the building up of Nauvoo, to a new home in Texas. At the death of Joseph, Brigham Young encouraged Lyman to not separate from the Saints, but he persisted and led the colony south which marked the end of his activity within the restored gospel. In subsequent years Lyman associated himself for a short time with the Reorganized Church surrounding Joseph Smith the Third, and then later rejected the call from the LDS Church in Utah for him to return to Salt Lake City. He was eventually excommunicated. Lyman died while seeking to return to Jackson County, which he still considered in his heart, as his Zion.

The Wild Ram

Wild Ram of the mountains, courageous bold
Dear friend to the prophet, was Lyman Wight
Through Jackson's oppression and prison cold
Shrunk not from the battle, fought the good fight

In Adam's great valley, he built his home
Adam-Ondi-Ahman's new branch he led
Called forth the militia, when mobs did come
Filled mobocrat hearts with fearing and dread

Expelled from Missouri, sent North to obtain
The lumber required, God's house to build
To Texas he fled, once Joseph was slain
To Brigham's counsel, his heart would not yield

Cut off from the Church, a victim of pride
Yet sought Zion's dream, 'til day that he died.

Oliver Cowdery

A common, even famous, leader among the Latter-day Saints, Brother Oliver Cowdery was with the prophet Joseph through many of the most sacred and significant events surrounding the restoration of Christ's church upon the earth. He was the Second Elder of the Church, serving second only to the Prophet Joseph Smith. He is still known as a special witness of the Book of Mormon, his name being affixed to every copy, as one of the three witnesses to that great scripture.

Oliver's difficulties with the Church seemed to begin at Kirtland Ohio, and his removal from there to Far West in September of 1837, did seem to occur under a cloud. In fact, in the same month Oliver moved to Far West, the Prophet Joseph Smith wrote concerning Oliver:

> "DEAR BRETHREN:-Oliver Cowdery has been in transgression, but as he is now chosen as one of the presidents or counselors, I trust that he will yet humble himself and magnify his calling, but if he should not, the Church will soon be under the necessity of raising their hands against him; therefore pray for him"[26]

While in Far West, Oliver took the responsibility to appoint additional lands for the gathering of the Saints, but in April 1837, charges against him were considered by a Bishop's council in Far West. Six of the nine charges that had been brought against Oliver were substantiated by the council and Oliver was disfellowshiped from the Church. Those six charges reveal some of what had happened to him. He was found to have persecuted the Saints with vexatious law suits, insinuated that the Prophet Joseph was an adulterer, shown contempt for the Church by not attending meetings, left his holy calling to practice law, disgraced the Church by bogus business practices, and finally..."*for leaving and forsaking the cause of God, and returning to the beggarly elements of the world and neglecting his high and holy calling, according to his profession.*"[27]

While Oliver did not appear at the Bishop's Council to answer the allegations, he did respond to them by letter. That letter, read in total, reveals great pride on the part of Oliver. Interestingly the main focus of his comments in that letter was to justify himself against the three charges that were not substantiated. With regard to all of the others, which were the cause of his being disfellowshiped, Oliver simply wrote; "*So far as relates to the other seven charges, I shall lay them carefully away, and take such a course with regard to them, as I may feel bound by my honor, to answer to my posterity.*"[28]

On that sad note, the influence and church activity of one of the great leaders of the early Church ended. Though thankfully, a more humble and repentant Oliver did later seek re-admittance into the Church and he was in fact re-baptized while the Saints were encamped at Winter Quarters. However, Oliver's experiences in Far West marked the beginning of a long and difficult separation for him.

2nd Elder

How hast thou fallen, from all thou hast known?
Who bowed beneath the hands of Elias

Beheld ancient records, by angel shown,
And denied not, in face of foul bias?

You wrote sweet words, that Joseph would reveal
Your God called you, just like his servant Paul
Witnessed Elijah grant power to seal
And the twelve, you were commissioned to call

Was pride at the core, as warned by your Lord?
Was it sickness, suffered in Far West's clime?
You'd not serve the Saints, nor grace, them afford
Lawsuits and lucre, replaced faith sublime

Yet, nigh unto death, your error realized
Meek, humble, at last, you were re-baptized

David Whitmer

Perhaps one of the more famous names from early Church history was David Whitmer, who, like Oliver Cowdery, was a special witness to, and whose name is still found in the introduction to, the Book of Mormon, Another Testament of Jesus Christ. He was the Son of Peter Whitmer Jr. at whose house the Church was first officially organized in 1830. He was baptized very early on in Church history. In fact, David was one of the original six members of the Church. When the Saints attempted to establish Zion in Jackson County, David Whitmer was called as president of the High Council and the Church in Missouri. His brother John Whitmer and William W. Phelps were called as his counselors.

When the Saints were expelled from Jackson County, David, John and William remained as the presidency over the Saints in Missouri and were serving as such at Far West. For a time David left Missouri and attempted to travel among the branches of the Church to encourage migration to Missouri. However, on April 13th, during the struggles and difficulties within the Church at Far West, David Whitmer was charged by the High Council with the following: failing to observe the word of wisdom, unchristian-like conduct, writing letters to Kirtland dissenters unfavorable to the cause and the character of Joseph Smith, neglecting his duties and sending an insulting letter to the council.[29] Earlier on President Whitmer had been relieved of his presidency by the high council, an action that he did not recognize, and he was no less adamant about what he considered to be the illegal nature of the High Council trying him for those mentioned charges. Though David Whitmer did not show up at the disciplinary council, he did send them a letter in which he outlined his strong feelings that the council had no right to try him and then, sadly, wrote;

> "Believing as I verily do, that you leaders of the councils have a determination to pursue your unlawful course at all hazards, and bring others to your standard in violation of the revelations, to spare you any further trouble I hereby withdraw from your fellowship and communion..."[30]

Tragically, David Whitmer never did return to fellowship in the Church, though he also never denied his testimony of the Book of Mormon.

Special Witness

"We, through the grace of God...have seen the plates"
Sweet witness proclaims, in your name declared
You moved with great faith across many states
With Saints seeking peace, their burdens you shared

Among Saints in Zion, called to preside
From Jackson to Far West, serving the Saints
Then abandoned the cause, made weak by pride
Withdrew from the Church, impugned their complaints

Unlike Oliver and Martin, you stayed
Aloof from the gospel, never returned
Yet, never denied, those claims you had made
E'n when you were mocked and your witness spurned

Dying outside the faith, but in God's hands
Of His precious plates, your witness still stands

William W. Phelps

A great and very talented early leader in the Church, and dear friend to the Prophet Joseph Smith, was William W. Phelps. Since Brother Phelps had experience in the field of publishing before joining the Church, much of his service in the Church was in that same area. In fact, in Jackson County he was the editor of the Evening and Morning Star. For a time he served as Joseph's personal scribe and his talents in writing are still apparent today in many of the well-known hymns of Zion including that spirit filled favorite, "The Spirit of God," which is still sung at all temple dedications.

As a counselor to David Whitmer in the Presidency at Far West, Brother Phelps was also caught up in the leadership turmoil of the times. In April of 1838, he joined with David Whitmer and John Whitmer in writing the letter denying the authority of the High Council to try them, and so refusing to appear, he was tried in absentia. The underlying issue in that disciplinary council was that he and John Whitmer had retained a $2,000.00 note subscribed for the building of the temple, and refused to release it to the Bishop, thus forcing the Bishop to pay a heavy mortgage thereon.

Upon leaving the Church, W.W. Phelps turned against his one-time friend Joseph, and was one of the few who visited with the mobocrat, General Lucas, just prior to the betrayal of Joseph at Far West. Brother Phelps also later testified against Sidney Rigdon in the Richmond trial, alleging that Sidney had engaged in Danite activities, and threatened to spill the blood of dissenters. However, to his credit, Brother Phelps later humbled himself and repented, seeking forgiveness from the Church. In a sweet and meekly written letter to the Prophet, sent from Dayton Ohio, Brother Phelps pled: ""*...I have seen the folly of my way, and I tremble at the gulf I have passed. So it is, and why I know not. I prayed and God answered, but what could I do? Says I, 'I will* repent and live and ask my old brethren to forgive me, and though they chasten me to death, yet I will die with them, for their God is my God...[31]

It is not revealed in the historical record, nor can we fully discern from his letter, what was going on in William Phelps' mind at the time of his betrayals. However, that his departure from the Church and turning against the prophet were a great pain to Joseph, is revealed in his letter written to Brother Phelps in response to the latter's request to rejoin the Saints. While no doubt reflecting on Brother Phelps departure and betrayal, Joseph wrote:

> It is true that we have suffered much in consequence of your behavior the cup of gall, already full enough for mortals to drink, was indeed filled to overflowing, when you turned against us. One with whom we had oft taken sweet counsel together, and enjoyed many refreshing seasons from the Lord, had it been an enemy, we could have borne it....[32]

Thankfully, true to the faith he professed, the Prophet Joseph, in spite of the pain and injustice he had suffered at the hands of Brother Phelps, still extended the hand of mercy and welcomed him back into the Church and fold of God. Today every time we sing William W. Phelps' hymn, "Praise to the Man," I cannot help but recall this event from history and my mind then calls to memory the last words of the Prophet's letter welcoming back brother Phelps, wherein he quoted these lines: "Come on dear brother, since the war is past, For friends at first are friends again at last."[33]

A Prophet's Friend

"The Spirit of God" great hymn from your heart
Inspired by God, through His spirit's power
How could you then fall, from such truths depart?
Who communed with Joseph, many an hour

Far West persecutions, were growing fierce
The prophet's cup of gall, filled to the brim
Made worse by your fall, his soul you did pierce
What anguish, when brother, turned against him

Yet he wrote, when you begged him to forgive
"Come on dear brother, since the war is past"
Those words filled your heart, caused your soul to live
"For Friends at first are friends again at last"

Once lost, now found "Praise to the Man" you penned
Died firm in the faith, prophet's loyal friend

Lyman Johnson

Lyman was an original member of the Quorum of the Twelve Apostles and well acquainted with the Prophet, in that for a time Joseph and Emma Smith resided at his home. Lyman Johnson served as a successful missionary in the early days of the Church and was a participant in the march of Zion's Camp. He was caught up in the initial difficulties surrounding the failure of the Kirtland Safety Society which challenged his faith, but was quickly reconciled to the Church and later moved to Far West.[34]

It was while he was at Far West that Lyman was charged with the misconduct which resulted in his being cut off from the Church. Among the charges that were brought against Lyman included sympathizing with dissenters, lying, and physical assault of another member. Though Lyman was never reunited with the Church, having moved to Iowa to establish a private law practice, he did still have some associations with the brethren, as late as July 1841, when he met with Joseph and other Church leaders at Nauvoo.[35] Sadly Lyman was drowned in a boating accident on the Mississippi River in 1856.[36]

What Profit

Called among the Twelve, Christ's special witness

Sent forth to all the world, to teach his word
Man of God, yet too, a man of business
By mammon hardened, 'gainst all he had heard

To warning voice, he refused to give heed
Sweet day of peace, spiritual communion
Made dim by anger, avarice and greed
Which soon destroyed, the once holy union

Far West, where council called him to explain
Humility, repentance had no part
Sought only then to hide the growing stain
Surrendered his soul, to a pride filled heart

Once light was gone, the way could not be found
Outside the faith he stayed, by Satan bound

Frederick G. Williams

This great leader and very close friend to the Prophet Joseph, was, like the others, baptized early on in the Church's history. He served many days as both a counselor and a scribe to the Prophet Joseph Smith. In a moment of sacred brotherhood, while participating with Joseph in the ordinance of washing of the feet, Brother Williams was moved upon by the Holy Spirit to display his loyalty and desires to remain faithful to the prophet in life. The History of the Church describes that sacred scene thus:

> *"At the close of the scene, Brother Frederick G. Williams, being moved upon by the Holy Ghost, washed my feet in token of his fixed determination to be with me in suffering, or in journeying, in life or in death, and to be continually on my right hand; in which I accepted him in the name of the Lord."*[37]

Frederick Williams also marched with Zion's Camp where he served as paymaster. Later, Brother Williams, a physician, was detailed to assist the people of Cleveland during a time of plague. In Kirtland he was appointed to be the editor of the Northern

Times. With the fall of the Kirtland Safety Society, Brother Williams was also caught up in the upheaval which plagued the whole Church. At one point he was brought to answer charges before the High Council in Kirtland, yet the angry words, and questions of authority resulted in the meeting ending in confusion. Later, however, some of the Saints raised objections to his serving as a counselor to the Prophet Joseph and he left Kirtland for Far West. In May 1838, while at Far West, Brother Williams' son died. It must have been a very difficult time for Brother Williams, and though the record is not clear as to what specific sins and transgressions were plaguing him, in an unpublished revelation given on July 8th just two months after the death of his son, the Lord speaks to both Frederick Williams and W.W. Phelps;

> "Verily thus saith the Lord, in consequence of their transgression their former standing has been taken away from them, and now if they will be saved, let them be ordained as Elders in my Church to preach my Gospel and travel abroad ..."[38]

That revelation seems to indicate that he had been cut off, and in August, Frederick was re-baptized and confirmed back into the Church. Sadly, his return was still under a cloud and as the persecutions upon the Church increased, and the Saints removed from Far West, he was eventually excommunicated by a council held in Quincy, Illinois on March 17, 1839.

A clue to what Brother Williams had undergone can be found in his affidavit prepared in March 1840, in which he certifies the he lost a considerable amount of land, buildings, etc. at Far West and that he was "compelled to leave the state under great sacrifice of real and personal property, which had reduced he and his family to a state of poverty."[39]

While he did not mention the death of his son and the other challenges to his faith, it is clear that he had truly passed through the refiner's fire. Thankfully his return to the Church was quickly accomplished. In April of 1840, in great humility, he presented himself before the Saints to ask forgiveness. Hyrum Smith then presented Brother William's case to the body of the Church which unanimously resolved that " Frederick G. Williams be forgiven, and be received into the fellowship of the Church.[40] Brother Williams died two years later of a lung ailment in the city of Quincy, Illinois, true in the faith and loyal to the Prophet.

Dear Friend

Brother Williams, our Prophets' dearest friend
Counselor and scribe, firm at Joseph's side
Desiring to prove faithful to the end
A momentary victim of your pride

Scandal, oppression and trials so sore
Weighed down at Far West, where you lost your son
Cut off from the Church, thus grieved all the more'
So humbled, turned back, to the Holy One

A wise prodigal, to Nauvoo you came
Seeking forgiveness, from your friends of old
At conference Hyrum presented your name
By each Saint welcomed, back into the fold

Oh he who so humbly washed Joseph's feet
With friend you now dwell, your mission complete

Orson Hyde

It is hard to believe that the well-known missionary who served so valiantly in England, and who later in his life was sent on a special mission to dedicate the Holy Land, could have had a period of apostasy. Yet at Far West, even though it was but for a short time, Orson Hyde did turn from the Church and even signed his name in support of the slanderous affidavit executed by Thomas Marsh. That affidavit exacerbated an already heated relationship between the Missouri mobs and the Latter-day Saints, and played a huge role in the eventual destruction of Far West.

Orson Hyde was called to the apostleship in February 1835, after returning from Zion's Camp, being set apart by Oliver Cowdery. In that beautiful ordination he was blessed with power to go to many nations, and was blessed to be even as one of the three Nephites.[41] In spite of the powerful promises he received, Brother Hyde did have some issues with the Church leadership. Later in the same year in which he was set apart, Brother Hyde presented a letter of complaint to the Prophet, complaining that he felt he was not being treated fairly, particularly in relation to the Prophet's brother William Smith, but upon conversation with the Prophet Joseph, he was satisfied on each of his concerns.[42] Orson Hyde then left for England to serve what was to be a very successful mission and was thus gone during the founding and initial growth of Far West.

However, in July of 1838, Elder Hyde arrived at Far West in company with Elder Heber C. Kimball who had been a fellow missionary with him in England. Strangely, in a period of just three months, Orson Hyde turned against the Church and as noted, affirmed some of the false assertions in Thomas Marsh's affidavit. There is no record as to what was going on in Orson Hyde's mind at the time, but in a commentary later written by President John Taylor, in which he adamantly denounces the Danite claims made by President Marsh, President Taylor, mentions that just prior to leaving the Church, Elder Hyde had suffered "with a violent fever for some time."[43] Those words seemed to have been written with the intent to allow for grace and compassion to be exercised upon Brother Hyde.

As a result of his action at Far West, Elder Orson Hyde was suspended from his office in the conference of May 1839 and given a charge to come forth at the next conference to account for his actions.[44] Elder Hyde did make his confession and in June of 1839 was restored to the priesthood.[45] Elder Hyde later spoke of his momentary separation at an open air conference in July of 1839 as the Prophet recorded:

> Elder Orson Hyde next came forward, and having alluded to his own late fall, exhorted all to perseverance in the things of God, expressed himself one with his brethren,

and bore testimony to his knowledge of the truth, and the misery of falling from it."[46]

What a powerful message from the very humble and repentant Elder Hyde. In October conference that year his restoration to the Quorum of the Twelve Apostles was ratified. He died in 1878 still firm in the faith.

The Olive Branch of Israel

Apostle to the Holy Land and Jews
Survivor of the tests of Zion's Camp
Great Teacher who, to England brought Good News
What Far West trial, dimmed your gospel lamp?

When flames of fury, fanned Missouri mobs
And Thomas swore to black and evil lies
While prairie air was filled with Saintly sobs
You certified their truth to all's surprise

Yet Fallen from your high and holy place
The sprit reached deep to your darkened soul
Then trusting in our Savior's bounding grace
You sought at Commerce Conference to be whole

To Twelve restored, then valiant you remained
And blessed the kingdom, love of Saints obtained

Thomas B. Marsh

Like many of the foregoing, Elder Thomas Marsh joined the Church early on in its history. Ordained to the quorum of the Twelve Apostles in February 1835, he was promised that he would be an instrument in bringing thousands of the "Lord's redeemed to Zion" and that angels would bear him up.[47] Later in April of that same year, he took his position as President of the Quorum of the Twelve Apostles and served for some time as its president.[48] As early as June 1837, President Thomas Marsh was granted land in Far West, even though at the time he still resided in Kirtland.[49] In the following month, the Lord through the Prophet Joseph, revealed His will to President Thomas Marsh, in which the Lord mentioned a few things in Elder Marsh's heart with which the Lord was not pleased, yet in that same revelation the Lord also blessed him.[50]

By November of 1837, Elder Marsh was in Far West and participated with the Prophet Joseph in reorganizing and settling the disputes and other affairs of the Church. It was during that time that he raised his voice against Frederick G. Williams.[51] As the difficulties in Far West began to increase, Elder Marsh was assigned as the President Pro Tem of the Church at Far West. While at Far West, Brother Thomas' 14 year old son James G. Marsh died.[52] Though not much is recorded about what else happened to Elder Marsh during the trials and dealings with the mob at Far West, it is clear in the record that it was at the height of the mob violence that Elder Marsh turned against the Church and swore out an affidavit in which he claimed that there were Danites, and what he termed the "destruction company" among the Saints and that the Prophet had claimed to be as a second Mohammad who would fill the country with blood.[53] The already angry mob was whipped into a frenzy by that affidavit and it was in part responsible for the terrible suffering of the Saints at the hands of the thus enraged mob. The allegations from that document also provided support for the claims that eventually led to the imprisonment of the Prophet and others in Liberty Jail.

As with some of the other leaders from Far West, Elder Marsh was excommunicated at the Quincy Conference in March of 1839, after which he remained outside the Church for many years.[54] Finally, 19 years later, Thomas Marsh rejoined the Saints and was re-baptized. Soon after his reunion with the Church, Brigham Young gave Brother Marsh an opportunity to speak to the Saints in which he related the following teachings, which give great insight into why so many of the Far West leaders had turned against the Church in its time of trial and which serves as a warning to any Saints who feel they are somehow beyond apostasy.

"If there are any among this people who should ever apostatize and do as I have done, prepare your backs for a good whipping, if you are such as the Lord loves. But if you will take my advice, you will stand by the authorities; but if you go away and the Lord loves you as much as he did me, he will whip you back again. Many have said to me, How is it that a man like you, who understood so much of the revelations of God as recorded in the Book of Doctrine and Covenants, should fall away?' I told them not to feel too secure, but to take heed lest they also should fall; for I had no scruples in my mind as to the possibility of men falling away."

"I can say, in reference to the Quorum of the Twelve, to which I belonged, that I did not consider myself a whit behind any of them, and I suppose that others had the same opinion; but, let no one feel too secure; for, before you think of it, your steps will slide. You will not then think nor feel for a moment as you did before you lost the Spirit of Christ; for when men apostatize, they are left to grovel in the dark." [55]

The True Prodigal

From early Saint, to quorum president
Endowed with power, in Kirtland's Holy Place
Our Savior's words through Prophet to you sent
A call to serve, and promise of His grace

Again the Lord spoke, to Zion you went
To pastor the flock, by Saints were approved
Then called at Far West, Pro Tem, President
Lost there a dear son, who you deeply loved

When wolves came to kill and scatter the flock
You turned on the Church, and evilly lied
The truths and doctrines once sweet, you did mock
Embraced Satan's power, perished inside

Thoroughly whipped, with the Saints you sought rest
Humble, re-baptized, joined them in the West

Isaac Russell

It is true that Isaac Russell is not a Saint whose name is immediately recognized by most Latter-day Saints, however, his story is compelling for two reasons. First, it is more common to the rank and file members of Latter-day Saints at the time, and thus speaks more to the general masses, and secondly because of an interesting and significant part he played surrounding the prophecy of Joseph Smith calling the Twelve to meet together and then leave for their missions from the temple lot in Far West, which was fulfilled on April 26,1839.

Elder Russell joined the Church in Canada, converted through the preaching of Elder Parley P. Pratt. He was also one of the early missionaries to England where serving under Heber C. Kimball, he did have success and actually organized a branch in Alston England.[56] While at Far West and in the height of its troubles, he turned from the faith and decided that he was to be the next Prophet of the Church to replace Joseph Smith whom he deemed as a fallen prophet. In December of 1838, while most of the faithful Saints were fleeing to Quincy Illinois, he led a band of Saints as the "Chosen of the Lord" westward, but at some point returned to the area of Far West.[57] In January of 1839, Isaac Russell wrote what he intended to be a secret letter, to the Saints he had taught and organized in England. In that letter he proposed to be a leader of the Saints in establishing Zion, claimed he possessed some special knowledge only meant for he and a few faithful, and warned them not to believe any reports that he had apostatized from the faith. Elder Richards, in England at the time, interceded with the Alston Saints and convinced them of Elder Russell's errors, and they remained faithful to the Church, though they grieved for their beloved mentor.[58]

In April of 1839, Elder Russell was still living with his wife in the vicinity of Far West. It was at the early morning meeting of the twelve (conducted in fulfillment of Joseph's prophecy to re-lay the temple cornerstone and prepare to go from there to their missions to the isle of the sea), in which Elder Russell and his wife were officially cut off from the Church.[59] The significant part they played came as the Twelve left for their missions in fulfillment of that prophecy. Elder Turley and company stopped by the house of Isaac Russell for the purpose of informing him that the revelation was in fact correct, and had been fulfilled. A detailed description of the meeting follows in Appendix A, and forms the basis of a limerick on life in Far West, which explains how shocked Isaac Russell was to learn that the prophecy he thought could never be fulfilled, actually was. Elder Turely's visit must have had an impact on his family, for soon after Elder Russell's death, his wife, who was also a witness to the fulfilling of the prophecy, migrated with her family to join the Saints in Utah.[60]

The Alston Elder

God's messenger of hope to English soil
Beloved by Alston Saints, 'mong whom you dwelt
Sustained by God, through all your British toils
Communion sweet with Christ, you must have felt

But British Saints, though tried, had not yet seen
The soul stretching trials, Far West did hold
The painful wrath of Satan, made so keen
Deceived your heart, toward Joseph made you cold

Self-proclaimed messiah, to Saints so blind
Professed God's call, that you Zion redeem
With heart made dead, a victim to your mind
And other's motes, made larger by your beam

Though you died, victim to Abraham's test
In time your family, joined Saints in the west

Brigham Young

Though the faith of many of the prominent Saints melted in the fervent heat of the Far West trials, there were many others who did not give way, and who remained steadfast and loyal to the Prophet and his call. Foremost among them was Brigham Young. Just as he had done in Kirtland, during the troubles in Far West Brother Brigham denounced the apostates and defended the prophetic call of Joseph Smith with all his heart. In fact, Brigham was only at Far West because he had to flee from the constant threats the apostates leveled against him at Kirtland. The Prophet Joseph recorded:

> "On the morning of the 22nd of December, 1837, Brother Brigham Young left Kirtland in consequence of the fury of the mob spirit that prevailed in the apostates who had threatened to destroy him because he would proclaim publicly and privately that he knew by the power of the Holy Ghost, that I had not transgressed and fallen as the apostates declared."[61]

Brigham Young's fierce loyalty served him well and he never did waiver. After the Prophet was arrested and the city of Far West was ransacked, Brigham was a huge force in assisting the Saints to flee the state, taking a prominent role in planning and then organizing the Saints for that purpose. Brigham remained in Far West assisting the poor and destitute Saints to flee, until he was forced to leave by the mob as later recorded; *"The persecution was so bitter against Elder Brigham Young (on whom devolved the presidency of the Twelve by age, Thomas B. Marsh having apostatized) and his life was so diligently sought for, that he was compelled to flee..."*[62]

Brigham Young, who was later designated the "Lion of the Lord," led the Church to Utah after the Prophet's martyrdom, built cities and colonized a huge portion of the west, including Utah, and died with the name of his prophet on his lips. Brother Brigham Young is a reminder to us all that it is possible to pass through deep trials and severe persecutions without surrendering to the powers of

Satan, or losing our witness as to the truths of the gospel. He truly was a Lion of the Lord.

Lion of the Lord

Oh Brother Brigham, Joseph's faithful friend
Named by one who knew, Lion of the Lord
Never wavering, valiant to the end
Defending truth, with spirit laden sword

When weaker Saints succumbed to Satan's power
Denied the faith, impugned the Prophet's call
With Lion's roar you made apostates cower
Stood firm in the faith, at risk of your all

When Liberty, your prophet kept confined
You organized the Saints who Far West fled
To help the poor, by oath you Saints did bind
With wisdom, from the state, by you were led

True to Joseph and God, through life and death
The name of Joseph graced your dying breath.

Thus, end the sonnets reflecting the lives of some prominent Church leaders who were caught up in the crucible of Far West. It is important to note that while some of the sonnets may seem harsh or judgmental, they were, in fact, written with a sense of wonder, some fear, and even a pleading desire for others to learn from the past and not let the comparatively weak and simple trials that we face in our day, lead us to apostatize from this true gospel or deny the faith that burns by spirit's light within the soul. We should truly have only respect and sorrow for the leaders who fell and did not return. Yet we should also have a deep sense of hope for them. That hope is based on the events surrounding the sweet experience already related about Frederick G Williams and deals with the doctrine of calling and election.

It is not the intent of this book to expound upon the doctrinal and scriptural truths behind the concept of having one's Calling and

Election made sure, only to point out that some of those who left the Church, and did not return in this life, may, by that doctrine, still be heirs to exaltation and eternal life in the worlds to come. Speaking of the same meeting in which Frederick Williams showed his great love for the Prophet by washing his feet, the Prophet Joseph later recorded:

> *"I then said to the Elders, As I have done so do ye; wash ye, therefore one another's feet; and by the Power of the Holy Ghost, I pronounced them all clean from the blood of this generation; but if any of them should sin willfully after they were thus cleansed,* **and sealed up unto eternal life***, they should be given over to the buffetings of Satan (until the day of redemption)."*[63]

For those familiar with the doctrine of calling and election, it seems clear by the foregoing account that those present were blessed with that gift on that sacred occasion. The importance of that event to this chapter is simply this; among the group so cleansed and sealed up was Lyman Johnson who therefore, though he never returned, may yet be an heir to exaltation.

Chapter Six

The Danites

It was within the trying and violent times of Far West that the sometimes still touted claim of the existence of Danites among the Saints first began. Its birth is entwined with the rebellions and misplaced zeal of a relatively new member of the Church who was living at Far West, Dr. Sampson Avard. While his organized movement was a failure and quickly extinguished, it formed a large part of the damaging affidavit of Thomas B. Marsh, verified in part by Orson Hyde, as mentioned in the previous chapter. That affidavit, and the actions of Avard, convinced many of the mob that there were actually Danites among the Saints, and justified them in their own minds, in the angry and vile retribution that they poured out upon the Far West Saints. Though never really a viable movement, the claims of its power and threat grew until it took on a life of its own and became the scapegoat for all the pretend evils that the conspiracy minded mobs were aching to believe existed among the hated Mormons. Interestingly, much like Joseph's "money digger" title, the Danite myth still lives today and is a popular challenge among the conspiracy hungry Anti-Mormons of our day who continue to seek to persecute the Saints.

Joseph Smith and John Taylor, who were both in Far West at the time, and who had personal knowledge of the truth about the alleged Danite movement, help to clarify what really happened, and what the Danites really were. The Prophet Joseph mentions that in the time of fear and apprehension among the Far West Saints, with mob action increasingly threatening their homes, the Saints had organized into self defense groups. In that dangerous and stressful time, Satan saw an opportunity to also attack the Church from within. Joseph wrote;

> "...while the evil spirits were raging up and down in the state to raise mobs against the "Mormons" Satan himself was no less busy in striving to stir up mischief in the camp of the Saints: and among the most conspicuous of his willing devotees was one Doctor Sampson Avard..."[64]

Joseph further details how Dr. Avard, with the intent to overthrow the Church and take power for himself, quietly began to meet with and initiate members into his band which he called Danites. With his promises of great glory to soon burst upon the Saints, and working in secrecy enforced by oaths and penalties of death, and even more damaging, with allusions to having the support of the Church leaders, Dr. Avard was able to make some headway among the Saints. His initial success had to also be related to the hopes of many Saints to see the persecutions of the mob thrown down and peace to be established once and for all. Dr. Avard actually organized his band into captains of tens and fifties and taught the initiates to be loyal to and strictly follow the directions of their captains. However, it was not long before he went too far.

In October of 1837 Dr. Avard called his captains to a secluded place to teach them what their mission would be. In a vile and angry speech, he proposed that the Danites would rob and plunder their "Gentile neighbors" and then informed them that they were to swear to an oath to lie and murder if necessary, to protect each other. That speech was his undoing, as all of Dr. Avard's supposed officers revolted and refused to go against the teachings of the Church and the laws of the land. Dr. Avard's miscalculation led to his activities coming to light and he was immediately cut off from the Church. Additionally, active measures were taken by the Church leaders to counter his influence among the Far West Saints.[65] In concluding his account of the Avard issue, and striving to clearly delineate between the Avard Danites, and the Far West work companies, the Prophet Joseph wrote:

> "Therefore, let no one hereafter, by mistake or design, confound this organization of the church for good and righteous purposes, with the organization of the "Danites" of the apostate Avard, which *died almost before it had existed*."[66]

For those who know by the Holy Spirit that the Prophet Joseph was and is a holy Prophet of God, his explanation above is sufficient and we can discount the Danites for what they were. However, since there are many who still long to see conspiracy and drama within the Church and who impugn the Prophet Joseph and wish to believe that Joseph's account of Avard was in error, particularly in light of apostate Thomas Marsh's angry affidavit, it is appropriate here to review the testimony of another witness to these affairs. On one occasion, after expressing a merciful hope that some of what the Thomas Marsh affidavit alleged had been added by the enemies of the Church and that it was not wholly the work of Marsh or Hyde, President John Taylor, went on to write:

> "...I was in Far West at the time these affidavits were made, and was mixed up with all the prominent church affairs. I was there when Thomas B. Marsh and Orson Hyde left there; ...and I know that these things referred to in the affidavits **are not true**. I have heard a great deal about the Danites, but I never heard of them among the Latter-day Saints."[67]

The eyewitness accounts of Joseph Smith and John Taylor should be enough for the honest in heart, yet the enemies of the Church who habitually look for evil within it, much like the Missouri mob in that day, will still use the Danites to further their own purposes.

Beware the Danites

Of all the goblins, ghost and ghouls
More fearful than the fiend who drools
Worse than the beast, who o'r hell rules
There stands the fearful Danite

Though never truly heard or seen
By rumor made more vile and mean
'Tis nothing makes one's fears more keen
Than that there Mormon Danite

O'r peaceful set'lers they have trod
Buried their children, under sod
And dun it, in the name of God
Beware the fearful Danites

Modern Mohammad at their head
They'll hunt us down, 'til we're all dead
And flood our land with blood so red
God save us from the Danites

Though never did a one we see
A fearsome lot, they all must be
Who've bragged that they'll burn Liberty
Oh we must stop the Danites

Dem Mormons say it isn't so
But we've heard from the ones who know
Dissenters swear with face aglow
They've fled from deadly Danites

If they're a myth, we do not care
The claims give us a power rare
Of Mormon's homes and lands we'll share
By saying there are Danites

In future days, histr'y will sigh
Condone us based upon that lie
And Anti-Mormons still will cry
"The Church was filled with Danites"

But wisdom, shall be justified
God will condemn all those who've lied
With Avard groveling at His side
He'll say.... "Behold the Danite"

Chapter Seven

The Church's Political Motto

It was in early March of 1838 that the Prophet Joseph Smith in company with Brigham Young, Daniel Miles and Levi Richards arrived in Far West after a long journey from Kirtland. Joseph recorded in his journal the joy with which he was received by the Saints at Far West, a joy made sweeter by the fact that he had experienced such bitter persecutions among false brethren at Kirtland. Having been thus welcomed to what he termed "the Saints' little Zion," he and his family boarded in the home of Brother George Harris, who willingly took him in and provided for his needs. About three days after Joseph's arrival, his Brother, Samuel Smith, arrived at Far West with his family. In this brief moment of rest and peace, there came to the Prophet's mind what he titled; *The Political Motto of the Church of Latter-day Saints.* The short paragraph which contained the motto outlined his feelings about liberty and included a reflection upon the debt owed to those who had fought in the past to secure our freedom. It was signed by the Prophet Joseph, his brother Samuel, and several other prominent members at Far West, including Thomas B. Marsh, Brigham Young and David W. Patten.[68]

Though the motto is short, it speaks powerfully and prophetically to the irony of a church founded on principles of liberty, and populated with many who had fought for, risked all for, the liberty of their nation, only to be denied that same liberty by a number of their fellow citizens. The following motto, (in bold letters), with all its power and irony, was later included in a letter from Joseph Smith to the Saints at Kirtland.[69]

<u>**The Political Motto of the Church of Latter-day Saints**</u>
<u>*(with poetic commentary)*</u>

The Constitution of our country formed by the Fathers of liberty.

They held those truths self-evident
From citizen to President
Each Soul endowed by God's own hand
With rights made sure on Promised land

Yet evil seeks to kill what's free
Cast down, destroy, all liberty
Thus government must wield some power
To bad contain; and good empower

So constitution they brought forth
Two centuries have proved its worth
Secured thereby sweet liberty
For us and our posterity

Peace and good order in society. Love to God and good will to man.

Our Jesus is the Prince of Peace
And when he comes, all strife will cease
Love for each soul will then increase
Thus Zion will be born

All good and wholesome laws, virtue and truth above all things, and aristarchy,[70] live forever!

Good laws proceed forth from good men
As wholesome fruit from wholesome trees
Bad statutes, will the wicked pen
As fig from thorns, one never sees

But woe unto tyrants, mobs, aristocracy, anarchy and torryism, and all those who invent or seek out unrighteous and vexatious law suits, under the pretext and color of law, or office, either religious or political.

What great reward will tyrants know?
What to all anarchists will flow?

What will God on all mobs bestow?
God has declared.......It shall be woe!

Exalt the standard of democracy!

Raise high the banner, o'r this land
Title of Liberty
Let all who read its symbols clear
Support democracy

Down with that of priestcraft, and let all the people say Amen! that the blood of our fathers may not cry from the ground against us. Sacred is the memory of that blood which bought for us our liberty,

Priestcrafts which killed that faith of old
Eroded nations sapped their strength
Now threaten us with actions bold
Make dark our nation's breadth and length

Oh God from priestcraft set us free
Preserve our blood bought liberty

Signed: **Joseph Smith, Jun., Tomas B. Marsh, David W. Patten, Brigham Young, Samues (sic) H. Smith, George M. Hinckle, John Corrill, George Robinson.**

DOCTRINE AND COVENANTS

OF

THE CHURCH OF THE

LATTER DAY SAINTS:

CAREFULLY SELECTED

FROM THE REVELATIONS OF GOD,

AND COMPILED BY

JOSEPH SMITH Junior,
OLIVER COWDERY,
SIDNEY RIGDON,
FREDERICK G. WILLIAMS.

[Presiding Elders of said Church.]

PROPRIETORS.

KIRTLAND, OHIO.

PRINTED BY F. G. WILLIAMS & CO.

FOR THE

PROPRIETORS

1835.

Chapter Eight

Revelations at Far West

While at Far West and vicinity, the Prophet Joseph Smith received eight revelations from the Lord, many of which have since been canonized as sections 113 through 120 of the Doctrine and Covenants. While the overall number of revelations is small compared to those arising out of Kirtland, the revelations that were received at Far West were very significant, and had a huge impact on the Church of Jesus Christ of Latter-day Saints, an impact that continues to this day.

Section 113

In March of 1838, soon after writing the Political Motto of the Church of Jesus Christ of Latter-day Saints, and while still at Far West, the Prophet Joseph wrote down the answers to some questions that had arisen from the writings of that great prophet Isaiah. While the ancient prophet Nephi delighted in the clarity of Isaiah, for many others, understanding the meaning of the revelations from that great Old Testament prophet is still a challenge. It is no doubt that the Prophet Joseph Smith had received some of the interpretations of Isaiah's symbols by revelation and thus his answers are canonized into the Doctrine and Covenants as Section 113.

Isaiah Explained

Son of Amoz, to Israel prophesied
Of Jesse's stem, his root and rod
And Zion's call to strength
Joseph made clear
That Saint's will rule at length
Prophets from Joseph, son of God
Isaiah's meaning by Prophet supplied[71]

Section 114

On April 17, 1838, The Lord revealed to the Prophet Joseph Smith at Far West, His will concerning one of the great apostles of the Church, who was also among the first martyrs for the restored Church of Jesus Christ, Elder David W. Patten. While more will be written about Elder Patten in Chapter Fifteen which covers the end of his life and his actions at the Battle of Crooked River, it is important here to note that this revelation called for Elder Patten to prepare for a mission with the Twelve. Thus, this Section is sometimes cited by Anti-Mormons -who carry on today the work once done by the Missouri mobs- as proof that Joseph Smith was not a prophet. Of course, the revelation proves nothing of the sort.[72]

Additionally, it is relevant to the Latter-day Saints, that the death of David Patten, in defense of his brethren, does not mean that he did not serve a mission. For those familiar with Section 138 of the Doctrine and Covenants, it is clear that Elder Patten actually did, and continues to, serve as a missionary for the Lord.

> *I beheld that the faithful elders of this dispensation, when they depart from mortal life, continue their labors in the preaching of the gospel of repentance and redemption, through the sacrifice of the Only Begotten Son of God, among those who are in darkness and under the bondage of sin in the great world of the spirits of the dead.*[73]

Thus, Elder David W. Patten, early martyr for Jesus Christ, hero of the Battle of Crooked River, and faithful apostle to the Church of Jesus Christ in Far West, is in every sense of the word a missionary.

The second portion of this short revelation is the Lord's powerful and plain warning to those who are called to positions of leadership within the Church and who thereafter deny His name. The result for such apostates is clear, for just as was manifested in the lives of those earlier mentioned leaders who apostatized from the Church during the Far West period, another will be called to receive their bishopric.

His Ways

*For a mission in the Spring
My servant David, should prepare
To the world his message bring
His Apostolic witness share*

*Like with King Hezekiah's plea
God changed his mind and Holy will
And he who died for liberty
Will in the next life, his call fulfill*

*And those among the sheep
Who turn from God, his name deny
Shall not their callings keep
Oh hear your Savior's warning cry*

*So many lost their Bishopric
Saw others called, to fill their place
And left to kick against the prick
Fell from the truth, shunned God's pure grace*

Section 115

On April 26, 1838 the Lord made known by revelation to His prophet Joseph Smith, His will concerning the building up of Far West as a holy and consecrated land. Significant in this revelation is the fact that through the Church's history, up to the time of this revelation, the Church had gone under, or been referred to by, several different names including; Latter-day Saints, Church of Christ, etc. However, in this revelation, the Lord made known what the official name of the Church would be. In verse four the Lord reveals: "For thus shall my church be called in the last days, even The Church of Jesus Christ of Latter-day Saints."[74]

Additionally, as already outlined in detail in Chapters Three and Four of this work, Section 115 makes it clear that Far West was no ordinary spot of ground. Though the Saints had already proceeded to prepare the ground for the building of a temple when Joseph received this revelation, it was not until he received it that the Saints began in earnest unity to lay the cornerstones and gather funds for the building of the Lord's House in Far West, this revelation providing a powerful endorsement of the Lord upon their previous desires and actions.

The final verse of this great revelation is somewhat prophetic, as it testifies that the Prophet Joseph held the keys of this kingdom, and that the Lord planned to sanctify him before the people. It was but one year later that the Prophet, sanctified through the trials of the temple prison in Liberty, received Sections 121 and 122 of the Doctrine and Covenants.

Finally, the last verse of this revelation sends a clear message from God, to the apostates in Kirtland and elsewhere, that Joseph was not a fallen prophet, and that he still held the keys.

After my Name

The Saints who dwelt at Far West
  By God had been richly blessed
    Who hearing prophet's request
      Named Church in manner so grand

Gather in Zion to me
  Safety and refuge you'll see
    From "wrath without mixture" flee
      To Far West my holy land

Let Saints of God gather 'round
  Let workmen of faith be found
    On Far West's most holy ground
      A house to your God must stand

Upon the prophet rely
   Whom your God will sanctify
      And keys, He will not deny
         Giv'n by God's almighty hand

Section 116

While the following chapter will outline in detail the Prophet's actions and revelations with regard to the establishment and naming of Adam-Ondi-Ahman, Section 116 provides the Lord's revelatory backing to all those prophetic utterances, and the explanation behind the deep affinity that the Saints in the Far West area gained for that sacred and holy spot of ground which was found just 17 miles to their north. This revelation was given while the Prophet was visiting Lyman Wight at his home near the beautiful Grand River.

<u>Spring Hill</u>

Spring Hill forgotten spot of earth
What is your destiny?
Christ, Adam, Saints will there meet in
Solemn Assembly

Section 117

The 8th of July of 1838 was a remarkable day for the Prophet Joseph, for the many revelations that he received at Far West. Section 117 was one of those revelations, and had the specific focus of revealing the Lord's will concerning several of the brethren, William Marks, Newel K. Whitney, and Oliver Granger. These brethren, who had been faithful servants and friends to the Prophet Joseph, were still living in Kirtland and by this revelation, they were directed to settle up their affairs in Kirtland and move to Far West. In the case of the first two, they were directed to do so before the snows fell. Apparently, Newel Whitney and William Marks were suffering from too much affinity for their lands and possessions in Kirtland, as in this revelation the Lord rebukes them for it.

As the revelation proceeds, the Lord mentions a name that occurs only once in scripture in this form, Olaha Shinehah, defined as the land were Adam dwelt. While Adam-Ondi-Ahman was becoming much more well known as the place where Adam or the ancient of days would return, Olaha Shinehah has little other mention. The Book of Abraham mentions Shinehah as meaning the sun.[75] Olaha however, is not mentioned anywhere else in scripture, though in the same verse in which God tells Abraham that the term Shinehah indicates the sun, He uses Olea, as a term for the moon, and some have hypothesized a relationship between those words. Whatever the translation of the name, it is clear that it represents the land where Adam lived, and most importantly for this book, it was in the vicinity of Far West.

While William Marks is called in this revelation, to go to Far West to "preside" among the Lord's people, Newel Whitney is warned to be ashamed of what the Lord calls the Nicolaitane Band. Nicolaitans are referred to by John in his revelation, and are deemed to be apostate Christians who adopted pagan beliefs forbidden by the early Christian Church leaders.[76] Elder Bruce R. McConkie describes Nicolaitans within the LDS Church as, "members of the Church who [are] trying to maintain their church standing while continuing to live after the manner of the world. . . The designation has come to be used to identify those who want their names on the records of the Church, but do not want to devote themselves to the gospel cause with full purpose of heart."[77]

In the final portion of this revelation, the Lord speaks to Oliver Granger, who is called upon to contend for the redemption of the first presidency, called to Zion to be a merchant, and directed to help hold up the prophet as one whom no man should despise.[78] Thankfully only one of these three men did not remain faithful to the restored Church. William Marks separated from the Church after Joseph's martyrdom and later became a counselor in the presidency of the Reorganized Church, now Community of Christ church.[79] However, Newell K. Whitney stayed faithful in the Church and served many years as a Bishop, not only in Far West, but in Nauvoo and later in the Presiding Bishopric in Salt Lake

City. [80] Oliver Granger faithfully served and fulfilled his assignments. He died before the Prophet Joseph, and was buried in Kirtland, where he was fulfilling his assignments to dispose of Church lands.[81] It is interesting that Oliver was promised in this revelation that his name would be remembered, and section 117 brings about fulfillment of that very promise, not only for him, but for the other two brethren who shared in this personal revelation from God.

Marks, Whitney & Granger

My son William, give heed to me
*A*wake, arise, to Far West come
*R*uler o'r many you shall be
*K*irtland no more, will be your home
*S*o come, it shall be well with thee

----

*W*ake up, my son, 'tis time to go
*H*ave faith, to sell your property
*I*n Zion's mount, your faith will grow
*T*here Shinehah's plains, your eyes may see
*N*icolaitane secrets I know
*E*scape their little souls, be free
*Y*es come, you'll reap of all you sow!

----

*G*enerations thy name shall hold
*R*emembered for thy sacrifice
*A*ct to redeem, contend, be bold
*N*o man shall e'r thy name despise
*G*ather to Zion, before the cold
*E*ngage in selling merchandise
*R*eceive those blessings now foretold

Section 118

In response to the Prophet Joseph's plea to know the will of the Lord concerning the Twelve, the Lord gave him what has become Section 118 of the Doctrine and Covenants. This revelation was also given on the 8th of July and provides specific guidance to the apostles. Most significant of this section is verse five, which, as outlined in other parts of this book, constituted the Lord's revelation concerning his will that the Twelve meet at the building site of the Far West Temple prior to their leaving on their assigned missions. When the revelation was given it did not seem like it would be a strange or wondrous thing to have happen, since their hopes were high for a peaceful and prosperous future. Yet since the Saints were driven from Far West in the months following the revelation and were dispersed long before the date that was appointed for this revelation to be fulfilled, that it was even fulfilled at all became a marvelous thing. In fact, in some instances the mob as part of their persecution tactics tried to use the prophecy as it is contained in verse five, combined with the fact that fulfillment then seemed humanly impossible, to prove to their victims that Joseph Smith was not a true prophet. On that point there is a powerful account recorded in the Church's history, which reveals not only the fulfillment of the revelation, but contrasts the difference between those who have faith in the fulfillment of revelations which appear unto man to be impossible to fulfill, and those who do not.

While Elder Turley was lingering in Far West as part of the committee for the removal of the remaining Saints from Missouri, one of the captains of the mob came to their meeting in company with the apostate John Whitmer, presented the revelation now contained in section 118, and gloatingly asked Brother Turley to read it.

> "Turley said: 'Gentlemen I am well acquainted with it.' They said, 'then you, as a rational man, will give up Joseph Smith's being a prophet and an inspired man?...' 'the twelve are now scattered all over creation; let them come here if they dare; if they do, they will be murdered. As the revelation cannot be fulfilled, you will now give up your faith.' Turley jumped up and said, 'In the name of God that revelation will be fulfilled."

In spite of his faith filled affirmations, the mob persisted in encouraging Brother Turley to be sensible and follow the course of other apostates. The record continues;

> Turley said, "Gentlemen, I presume there are men here who have heard Corrill say, that 'Mormonism' was true, that Joseph Smith was a prophet, and inspired of God. I now call upon you, John Whitmer: you say Corrill is a moral and good man; do you believe him when he says the Book of Mormon is true, or when he says it is not true? There are many things published that they say are true, and again turn around and say they are false?" Whitmer asked, "Do you hint at me?" Turley replied, "If the cap fits you, wear it; all I know is that you have published to the world that an angel did present those plates to Joseph Smith." Whitmer replied: "I now say, I handled those plates; there were fine engravings on both sides. I handled them;" and he described how they were hung, and "they were shown to me by a supernatural power;" he acknowledged all. Turley asked him, "Why is not the translation now true?" He said, "I could not read it [in the original] and I do not know whether it [i.e. the translation] is true or not." Whitmer testified all this in the presence of eight men.[82]

The story of Elder Turley's defense of this revelation, the Prophet Joseph Smith and the Church, is significant because the very revelation used by the mob on that occasion as proof of Joseph's fraud, was actually fulfilled in spite of the seeming impossibility of such a thing. As already described in portions of Chapters Four and Five and detailed in a limerick in the final chapter, true to this revelation, the Twelve did fulfill God's will. Section 118's powerful expression of God's will concerning the twelve, and call to some prominent brethren to step up and become apostles, as well as his pinpoint assignment of the time and place for the beginning of their missions, indicates to us all that God's plans and purposes are indeed intertwined with this Restored Gospel and will be fulfilled in His time and manner.

God's Will

Call forth a conference, at this very place
Replace the few, who've fallen from my grace

Let Thomas stay, and publish forth my word
While residue, share all that they have heard

For families, I'll open up the door
Blessings upon their heads from heaven pour

Next Spring, the Twelve, shall preach to Isles in need
From Temple lot, let that mission proceed

John Taylor with my servant John E. Page
Called to Apostleship, must then engage

Willard Richards, Wilford Woodruff shall too
Serve as Apostles, all my works to do

Sections 119 & 120

Like the preceding section, these revelations came as a direct response to an inquiry of the Prophet Joseph Smith and were also given at Far West. Together they formulate the law of tithing as it is still practiced in the Church today. Any who are familiar with the Church's current practices on tithing will understand and recognize the portion of this revelation that defines what constitutes a tithe, which is *"one tenth of all one's interest annually."*

God's Law

Will man rob God? So asked the Holy King
All who love me, their tithes will gladly bring

Saints at Far West, who seek to sanctify
And Zion build, must with this law comply

> *One tenth of all, your interest annually*
> *To build mine house, from debt my Church set free*
>
> *To Zion's stakes, ensample this shall be*
> *If lived in faith, shall make my Saints holy*
>
> *To be disposed, by council as ordained*
> *And by my voice, that peace you may obtain*

Other Far West Revelations

Not all of the revelations received by the Prophet Joseph Smith at Far West were canonized into the Doctrine and Covenants. There were two other revelations given, which had an impact on the Saints and their life at Far West, but which were never canonized. The first was given in April 1838, through Joseph Smith to the Apostle Brigham Young. As noted, Brother Brigham had fled Kirtland the preceding December in consequence of his faithful and valiant support of Joseph Smith, which in turn had endangered his life while he lived among the apostates. Thus Elder Young had only been in Far West for about three months. In this sweet and tender revelation to Brigham, the loving Lord said:

> *Verily thus saith the Lord, let my servant Brigham Young go unto the place he has bought, on Mill Creek, and there provide for his family until an effectual door is opened for the support of his family, until I shall command him to go hence, and not to leave his family until they are amply provided for. Amen.*[83]

This revelation, though not in the Doctrine and Covenants, is still sweet to any who have known the challenges of family separation, and calls to mind a later similar revelation wherein the Lord called Brigham to remain at home and care for his family.[84]

Brigham's Charge

How valiant in my cause you've been
Your family's paid the price
And suffered much for my name's sake
I've seen their sacrifice

Now you must stay, on Mill Creek's land
You need do nothing more
And lift your family, for whom soon,
I'll open up the door.

The second such revelation, like some of those just reviewed which are actually recorded in the Doctrine and Covenants, was given on the 8th of July, 1838. It was given through the Prophet Joseph and directed towards both William W. Phelps and Frederick G. Williams. As mentioned previously, it relates to their standing in the Church and is recorded in full;

> *Verily thus saith the Lord, in consequence of their transgressions their former standing has been taken away from them, and now, if they will be saved, let them be ordained as Elders in my Church to preach my gospel and travel abroad from land to land and from place to place, to gather mine elect unto me, saith the Lord, and let this be their labor from henceforth. Amen[85].*

As already mentioned, both these brothers were moved upon by the Spirit, repented of their weaknesses, returned to the Church, and died faithful. They were blessed because they had the humility and testimony sufficient to motivate them to set aside hard feelings and to give heed to these words of their Lord, and return to accept the sweet embrace of God's redeeming grace.

Return

Oh William, who from grace did fall
Will you not turn to me?

> *Though lost to you, Apostle's call*
> *An Elder you may be*
>
> *Frederick, whose pride your fall did cause*
> *Remove you from your place*
> *As Elder now obey my laws*
> *Take hold, receive my grace*

Joseph Smith History

Though not technically a revelation, it is important to note that it was at Far West that the Prophet Joseph Smith took time to record his official history, which now makes up a significant part of the Pearl of Great Price. That detailed and spirit-filled account of the first vision and subsequent manifestations surrounding the coming forth of The Church of Jesus Christ of Latter-day Saints, was written in May of 1838, in response to the many questions that Joseph had been required to answer. In the opening verse of that history, the Prophet explains his purpose; *"...I have been induced to write this history to disabuse the public mind, and put all inquires after the truth in possession of the facts."*[86] In his journal, the Prophet recorded that from May 1st through the 4th of 1838, he and the First Presidency at Far West spent their time *in writing the Church history* and ministering to the sick.[87] Interestingly, near the end of the Joseph Smith History itself, the prophet wrote speaking of the plates of gold;

> But by the wisdom of God, they remained safe in my hands, until I had accomplished by them what was required at my hand. When, according to arrangements, the messenger called for them, I delivered them up to him; and he has them in his charge *until this day, being the second day of May, one thousand eight hundred and thirty-eight.*[88]

There is no doubt that along with the mentioned revelations found in the Doctrine and Covenants, and those not canonized which were received at Far West, the precious scripture contained in the

Joseph Smith History also came to us from the holy place of Far West.

Joseph's History

His name would be had, for good and for bad
Among Nations, states, every land
So sweet now to hold, the truth as retold
Written by our dear Prophet's hand

God broke heaven's seal, his presence revealed
Joseph, saw and heard the beloved Son
Thus Emanuel, did darkness dispel
At long last, restoration had begun

To Joseph one night, came heavenly light
Moroni, the prophet of old
Who with trumpet sound, brought forth from the ground
Joseph's stick, revealed, as foretold

Then to Joseph's side, his God did provide
Companion, his calling to share
Blest richly his life, gave Emma as wife
Together, the burdens to bear

In poverty's power, at most desperate hour
The Lord did supply Joseph's need
Martin's kindly gift, his spirits did lift
Translation work, then could proceed

To prove it no fake, for Martin's own sake
To New York some copies he took
First Anton confirmed, but later affirmed
That he could not read a sealed book

Oh glorious day, that morning in May
John, from the heavens did descend
And priesthood restore, key, powers, once more
On earth, to remain, 'til the end

Chapter Nine

Adam-Ondi-Ahman

It was in the spring of 1838 that the Prophet Joseph in company with Sidney Rigdon, Thomas Marsh, David Patten and others headed Northward from Far West with the purpose of laying out other stakes of Zion. Their journey led them to the place already referred to in the last chapter as Spring Hill, which the Lord revealed to be Adam-Ondi-Ahman. As with those who have visited Far West, for many who have had the opportunity to visit this beautiful and serene valley near the Grand River, the sprit has born witness to their souls that it was not an ordinary place. In fact, the spirit witnesses to all who ponder over Adam-Ondi-Ahman that it is a sacred place with both historic, and future significance. While a direct translation of that name has never been given, it is clear that Adam refers to the Ancient of Days, the first man. Ahman appears twice in the Doctrine and Covenants and clearly refers to Jesus Christ. In section 78, after mentioning the land Adam-Ondi-Ahman, the Lord refers to himself as Son Ahman.[89] Similarly in Section 95, Jesus refers to himself as Son Ahman.[90] Thus the name Adam-Ondi-Ahman has clear reference to both the Savior Jesus Christ and Adam, the first man.

The many special purposes of that land, as revealed by the Prophet Joseph, are both exciting and interesting. For example, we learn that Lyman Wight had built his house at the foot of what the Prophet called tower hill, *"in consequence of the remains of an old Nephite altar or tower that stood there."*[91] Even more significant is the understanding that Adam-Ondi-Ahman was, and is still to be, a sacred place in the history of this earth. For as outlined in Section 107 of the Doctrine and Covenants we learn that it was at Adam-Ondi-Ahman where Adam gathered his posterity together not long before his death, and blessed them.

The scriptures record that though he was very old, the spirit came upon him and Adam prophesied of all that would befall his posterity throughout time. Most sacred to that historic meeting was the fact that the Lord himself appeared and comforted Adam. It is hard to imagine a more sacred or holy setting, yet that which is to take place in the last days will be just as sacred and beautiful. We learned from Section 116 that Adam-Ondi-Ahman is to be the place where Adam will come in the last days as spoken of by the mouth of Daniel the Prophet. In essence there is to be a large Priesthood gathering at that very valley, where Father Adam will stand before thousands and where the Savior of the world will come with the clouds of heaven to that sacred solemn assembly. Elder Bruce R. McConkie described it thus.

> ...There the prophet taught them that Adam again would visit in the valley of Adam-Ondi-Ahman, holding a great council as a prelude to the great and dreadful day of the Lord...At this council, all who have held the keys of authority will give an accounting of their stewardship to Adam. Christ will then come, receive back the keys, and thus take one of the final steps preparatory to reigning personally upon the earth.[92]

So much of the history and the future of our earth, as tied up in the life of Father Adam, was made manifest by Section 116. The simple words of that revelation bring clarity to the writings and prophecies of Daniel,[93] and fill the Saints with a hope for the joyous solemn assembly to come. These blessings are now ours because the Prophet Joseph Smith, under the inspiration of heaven, was led to go north from his home in Far West.

Go North

Go north, Go north to Eden's land
I've treasures for you there
Go north, my son, behold the place
That now you must prepare

Go north, Go north, and walk the earth
That once was Adam's home
Go north my son, look on the vale'
Where soon your Lord will come

Go north with faith, and find the rise
That shall be Adam's seat
When Son of Man and priesthood will
In solemn spirit meet

Go north, Oh see what Daniel Saw
The Ancient of all days
In garments white, on fiery throne
On whom the judgment lays

North to Spring Hill, where as revealed
Son Ahman shall appear
Receive the keys, dominions, powers
Go north...the time is near

Be clean Oh Priesthood of our God
Live pure, be sanctified
That in Diahman's valley then
Christ's presence you'll abide.

Adam-Ondi-Ahman

Chapter Ten

Blessing of the Children

On April 6, 1838, a significant day for the Missouri Saints by itself, and just two days after President Rigdon had arrived with his family at Far West, the Saints met in a General Conference. This conference was convened at the decision of the High Council at Far West in order to celebrate the anniversary of the Church and to conduct church business. It was also determined that as part of that conference, the Sacrament would be administered and a time would be reserved for the blessing of infants.

The record of that conference states; *"After one hour's adjournment, meeting again opened by David W. Patten. The bread and wine were administered, and ninety-five infants were blessed."*[94] It is true that by itself the statement is not amazing, and appears even routine in relation to what was done. However, the significance is found in the number of infants who were blessed at that conference. Upon closer reflection of how that event must have been carried off, any Latter-day Saint familiar with the procedure of blessing infants, would have to be impressed with such an event and the sweet spirit that would, no doubt, have attended it. Additionally, that there where ninety-five infants even present in the Far West settlement, is to all a witness as to the Saints' understanding and faith in the Lord's commandments and directions concerning families and the (still in force) command to replenish the earth.

A beautiful precedence of this sacred scene is recorded in the Book of Mormon relating to the Savior's blessing of the Nephite children. That blessing, accompanied by powerful manifestations of the Sprit and miracles among those blessed, is recorded in precious detail in 3 Nephi Chapter 17, and serves as a sweet reminder of God's love and tender mercies for the "little ones." That same love was manifested many years later at this conference in Far West.

The blessing of the infants at that April Conference also brings to mind a merciful and loving Father in Heaven who was preparing his children for trying times which He knew lay just ahead. Sadly, just a little over a year later, Far West would be abandoned, what's more, just a few months later, some of those infants who had been blessed on that day, were to face with their families extreme trials and hazards at the hands of a violent mob. As a result, some would even die. Yet others would survive to bring strength to a church in need. Either way, that day was significant and glorious for those ninety-five infants and the families who loved them.

Blessing of the Infants
April 6, 1838

Oh sacred scene, sweet day of grace
Saints first communed, then infants blessed
What power must have filled that place
Lifted the hearts, of those oppressed

Almost one hundred infants pure
Priesthood blessings and names received
By Fathers who would yet endure
Hate, for their faith, what they believed

How like that day, in Bountiful
When Jesus blessed each precious child
Broke Bread to sanctify each soul
Blest babes who spoke, with voice so mild

Yet Far West Saints, were not to know
Two hundred years of love and peace
The power of the mobs would grow
Proud persecutions but increase

Some of those Babes, were killed or died
As tiny martyrs for God's truth
Some others lived, Far West survived

Grew strong as mighty noble youth

Oh do not mourn, for infants dear
Blessed that day, in Zion's land
Each Father's plea our God did hear
Each child kept hallowed, in His hand

THE ELDER'S JOURNAL

OF THE CHURCH OF JESUS CHRIST OF LATTER DAY SAINTS;

EDITED BY

Joseph Smith jr.,

IS PRINTED AND PUBLISHED BY

Thomas B. Marsh,

AT $1 PER ANNUM IN ADVANCE.— EVERY PERSON PROCURING TEN NEW SUBSCRIBERS, AND FORWARDING $10 CURRENT MONEY, SHALL BE ENTITLED TO ONE VOL. GRATIS.— ALL LETTERS WHETHER FOR PUBLICATION, OR OTHER PURPOSES, MUST BE DIRECTED TO THOMAS B. MARSH, POSTAGE PAID. No subscription will be received for less term than one year.

Chapter Eleven

The Elder's Journal (Far West Edition)

While residing at Far West, the Saints did publish a periodical that was called the Elder's Journal. In fact, the Journal had first been printed in Kirtland, but the Anti-Mormon elements in Kirtland put a stop to it. Once the Prophet had left Kirtland and was situated in Far West, the Elder's Journal was published again with Thomas Marsh as publisher and Joseph Smith as editor. In the first Far West issue, the Prophet Joseph presented and then answered twenty questions, which he said he did in order to save him from having to repeatedly answer the same questions.[95] Apparently, the rumors and stories about him were so prevalent, that Joseph spent much of his time answering the same old allegations and to that end, he hoped by this action to relieve himself of that burden. Thus, he published before the world his answers to the most prominent ones.

Joseph's answers to those questions are succinct, or some might even say blunt, but by that same token, they are actually refreshing. There follows now a poetic recital, or summary, of his answers to those questions. The actual questions and answers as they appeared in the Elder's Journal can be read in total in Volume Three of the History of the Church.

20 Answers

Question One: Do you believe in the Bible?

If we believe the Bible's true
We are the only ones who do

Question Two: Wherein do you differ from other sects?

God's Holy Bible, Saints accept
But unlike Christians of our day

*We have no creeds to change precept
Don't just profess….. live what we say*

Question Three: Will everybody be damned but Mormons?

*The Mormon faith does hold the keys
Thus all must of its truths partake
Yet, being Mormon will not save,
Those who repentance do forsake*

Question Four: How and where did you obtain the Book of Mormon?

*Moroni, prophet from the past
To plates of gold my path did lead
Where they with Urim, Thumim, lay
That all the world might one day read*

Question Five: Do you believe Joseph Smith Jr. to be a Prophet?

*A testimony of God's Son
Doth fill my soul, and set me free
Thus prophet by God's word I am
For this spirit of prophecy*

Question Six: Do the Mormons believe in having all things in common?

*Though Mormons don't of all things share
For all our fellows we do care*

Question Seven: Do the Mormons believe in having more wives than one?

*We teach each man should have one wife
And cleave to her through all her life
Man may remarry, if spouse dies
But time should pass, before he tries*

Question Eight: Can they [the Mormons} raise the dead?

No Mormon, and no other man
Who've lived upon this mortal sphere
Had power alone to raise the dead
Or make the buried, God's voice hear

Yet God, with power over death
Can through the priesthood keys restored
Share sacred power, to raise the dead
With worthy servants of the Lord

Question Nine: What signs does Joseph Smith give of his divine mission?

What signs, Joseph, will you reveal
To prove your calling in our day

The signs God chooses in His will
To prove the world, in His own way

Question Ten: Was not Joseph Smith a money digger?

I dug for money, just as they say
But quit, it brought such little pay

Question Eleven: Did not Joseph Smith steal his wife?

Did Joseph steal his wife away?
Ask Emma, She'll have lots to say

Question Twelve: Do the people have to give up their money when they join the church?

How much of mammon, must one give
If Mormon they become
Enough to meet the kingdom's need
Provide the poor a home

Question Thirteen: Are the Mormons abolitionists?

To free from bondage all false priests
  Their souls from sin to save
Is abolition which we seek
  To free a different slave

Question Fourteen: Do they not stir up the Indians to war, and to commit depredations?

Do Saints stir up the native tribes?
To depredations cause
No, 'tis a lie, spun by vile men
The Saints respect our laws

Question Fifteen: Do Mormons baptize in the name of Joe Smith?

We baptize not, in Joseph's name-but as our Lord directs
Yet if we did, it'd be the same-as all the powerless sects

Question Sixteen: If the Mormon doctrine is true, what has become of all those who died since the days of the Apostles?

If Mormons have the truth restored
Brought back today in Jesus name
What of the millions of our Lord
Who died before this blessing came

Our God is just, and loves each child
Thus judgment on them he'll withhold
'Til all have heard his gospel mild
In life or death, his truths behold

Question Seventeen: Does not Joe Smith profess to be Jesus Christ?

I'm but a man, not God or Christ
Mere mortal, I profess none other

But this I know, as Jesus taught
To Christ the King, I am a brother

Question Eighteen: Is there anything in the Bible which licenses you to believe in revelation now-a-days?

Prove now that heavens are not sealed
Why think ye that our God still speaks?
No scripture has to us revealed
That God won't answer one who seeks

From all we've learned and all we've read
We know revelation isn't dead

Question Nineteen: Is not the canon of scripture full?

The Bible Canon is not full
For many books are missing still
Yet, God promised to all who seek
His heart and mind, He will reveal

Question Twenty: What are the fundamental principles of your religion?

Jesus is center of our faith
We, with all witnesses, proclaim
He died for us, but rose again
Hosanna to his precious name

We trust in gift of Holy Ghost
Believe that truth will yet prevail
That Israel's tribes will be restored
And power of faith, will never fail.

In that same edition of the Elder's journal, the Apostle David W. Patten wrote a beautiful and faith-filled discourse on the topic of the fullness of times. After outlining many scriptural references with regard to all the dispensations of the Gospel in the earth, Elder Patten provided two basic definitions for the meaning of the significant term *dispensation of the fullness of times*. First, midway through his discourse he wrote; *...what the fullness of times means or the extent or authority thereof. It means this, that the dispensation of the fullness of times is made up of all the dispensations that ever have been given since the world began, until this time.*[96] Later, after naming the heads or leaders of the dispensations of the past, he explains a bit more about this final dispensation with regard to the "deliverer" who will be called to lead it; *...for this it means, that all things shall be revealed both in heaven and on earth; for the Lord said there is nothing secret that shall not be revealed, or hid that shall not come abroad, and be proclaimed upon the house top, and this may with propriety be called the fullness of times.*[97]

In his concluding paragraph of that powerful discourse, Elder Patten gets to the heart and purpose of his message, which was to show that the Church was being led by the chosen men of God, with the authority of heaven to lead God's people in the dispensation of the fullness of times. Elder Patten's article was no doubt of great comfort to the Prophet Joseph, whose very presence in Far West at the time, was due in part, to the many apostates in Kirtland and other places who had turned against him and the Gospel. Perhaps with those very apostates in mind, Elder Patten concluded his discourse with this warning:

> Therefore, brethren, beware concerning yourselves, that you sin not against the authority of this dispensation, nor think lightly of those whom God has counted worthy for so great a calling, and for whose sake he hath made them servants unto you that you might be made the heirs of God to inherit so great a blessing, and be prepared for the great assembly, and sit there with the Ancient of Days, even Adam our father, who shall come to prepare you for the coming of Jesus Christ our Lord; for the time is at hand...[98]

Elder David W. Patten's pointed teaching about the fullness of times, his testimony and unfailing support of the Prophet Joseph and the other leaders of this final dispensation, were sealed by his blood just three months later, where in defense of the Saints at Far West, Elder Patten was killed in the Battle of Crooked River.

Fullness of Times

Dispensations for each age
By God have been proclaimed
Until the final, full one, comes
It's head by God was named

    Adam first after the fall
    Noah, father of us all
    Abraham, who heard God's call

    Moses, Israel's prophet bold
    Elias, as was foretold
    John, whom Herod sought to hold

    Jesus, who is king of kings
    Peter, keys of sealing brings
    Joseph, whom God gave all things

Hear now, ye sleeping sons of God
The Good News of your Lord
For all the keys, powers, rights have been
In these last days restored

Chapter Twelve

Growth of Persecution

Part One
Scuffle at Gallatin

The event that first focused the mobs' powerful anger and which in the end was to lead to the eventual expulsion of the Latter-day Saints from Far West and even Missouri, centered around a most basic of human rights, the right to vote. Not unaware of growing hatred against them, the Saints still planned to exercise their right to vote on election day, the sixth of August, 1838. A friend of the Church had warned the brethren of the mobs' intention of prohibiting the "Mormons" from voting in an effort to guarantee the local election of a mob leader. The friend warned that if the Saints intended to go to Gallatin, they should go armed and be prepared to fight for their right to vote, but the Saints, hoping that the warning was not in earnest, moved toward Gallatin without weapons, and with the intent to exercise their rights.[99]

Upon arriving at Gallatin, the brethren who wanted to vote were immediately harangued and insulted by the mob supported candidate, Pennington, who desired, for obvious reasons, that they not be allowed to vote. Those actions incited a large bully by the name of Welding, who was already under the influence of alcohol, to loudly proclaim, that neither "Mormons nor Negroes" would be allowed to vote in their county. The bully then tried to enforce his claim by attacking one of the brethren. That action, in turn, led to a general battle royal between the Saints and the mob, the Saints being outnumbered about ten to one. While the mob viciously attacked the members, and cried for their death, thankfully they had no weapons beyond boards, clubs and fists. As the battle and anger intensified, the mobbers left to acquire their lethal weapons so that they might have their way with the Saints. In the reprieve, though still strongly desiring to vote, the brethren determined it best for them to leave. Later that evening fearing reprisals from the mob, they moved their families from their homes to hide them in the fields and stood guard around them through a rainy night.[100]

In Far West, the Prophet Joseph received reports about what had happened in Gallatin, which included claims that some of the brethren had been killed, and he immediately left with a small group to try and support the disenfranchised Saints in Daviess County. It was with great relief that the rescue party later discovered that none of the Saints had actually been killed, though some had been pretty badly beaten. In his "after action" report of the events, the Prophet Joseph wrote this interesting summation:

> "From the best information we have about one hundred and fifty Missourians warred against from six to twelve brethren, who fought like lions. Several Missourians had their skulls cracked. *Blessed be the memory of those few brethren who contended so strenuously for their constitutional rights and religious freedom, against such an overwhelming force of desperadoes.*"[101]

It was from that sad day in Gallatin, that the Saints began to suffer more and more at the hands of the mob, until the infamous extermination order was given. How interesting it is to note that the mob's desires to disenfranchise the Saints and deprive them of a basic civil liberty which lay at the heart of the Gallatin incident so many years ago, still exists as a strident theme in the hearts and minds of the Anti-Mormons of our day.

The Scuffle

Don't go, the Saints were warned away
The mobs won't let you in
But Saints still sought to have their say
And moved toward Gallatin

Then Pennington, began to howl
The town's folk to incite
'Til bully Welding, drunk and foul
'Gainst Brown, began to fight

With clubs, with fists, and boards, the mob
The brethren, did assail
Who anxious to complete the vote
Sought to, o'r mob, prevail

"Kill Him, Kill Him" cries filled the air
When e'r Saint fought them back
At ten to one, the odds weren't fair
But still, mobs skulls did crack

Fought like lions, for liberty
Against those devil's sons
Yet Saints at last were forced to flee
When mobbers went for guns

Much fearing what the future brought
The Saints moved to defense
While growing mob, still angry, sought
Their greedy recompense

Part Two
Adam Black Affair[102]

Two days following the fracas at Gallatin, Joseph, at the head of his small force which had moved to Daviess County originally to assist the Saints, visited the Anti-Mormon judge Adam Black. Their intention was to get him to sign a document promising that, as judge, he would fairly treat the Mormons and set aside his mob leanings. He did, at length, write out his own statement and sign it, but no sooner had the Saints left, than he swore out a false affidavit accusing the Prophet and his men of threatening both himself and all other Missourians, claiming that the Mormons were holding at defiance the laws of the land. Judge Black's affidavit, along with subsequent supporting affidavits from the mob, formed the basis of the rationale used by the mob to seek for volunteers from the outlaying counties to gather with the intent of driving the Saints not only from Daviess County, but from Caldwell and Carroll Counties as well.

Additionally, it was his affidavit and allegations against Joseph and Lyman Wight, which led to their being arrested, though once the sheriff had arrested Joseph, he realized he had no jurisdiction and so he left. That simple act, in turn, fueled claims that the Mormons had usurped the law. The gathering of the mob and increased tensions led Governor Boggs to mobilize the militia to a "stand by" status to be ready to quell any disturbances that might arise.

In expressing his poignant feeling about all that the Saints had endured, his past memories being compounded by the current difficulties, the Prophet Joseph first spent some time recording all the they had innocently suffered, mentioning their submission to the many injustices that had preceded their move to Far West, and then poignantly wrote;

> ...We have not complained at the great God, we murmured not, but peaceably left all; and retired to the back country, in the broad and wild prairies, in the barren and desolate plains, and there commenced anew; we made the desolate places to bud and blossom as the rose; and now the fiend like race is disposed to give us no rest. Their Father the devil, is hourly calling upon them to be up and doing, and they like willing and obedient children, need not the second admonition...[103]

Eventually in an attempt to establish peace, Joseph and Lyman submitted to be tried by Judge King from Richmond, and though there was no evidence presented against them, they were still held over on a $500.00 bond. At this point the mob attacks on the Mormons living in the outlying areas were beginning, and there was a rumor that the mob was gathering to attack Adam-Ondi-Ahman. In response to those rumors, some of the brethren from Far West left for Adam-Ondi-Ahman to help defend the Saints there.

Captain Allred from the Caldwell Militia in Far West led another group of mounted brethren to intercept a shipment of guns they had heard rumors about. Allred's company actually found a broken down wagon, and the weapons were discovered in a hastily camouflaged pile on the ground. As Allred's group was investigating that peculiar scene, another group of men with a replacement wagon arrived. It was clear to all present, that the weapons were intended to arm the mob, and so, brother Allred, under authority of the judge in Far West, arrested the mob members, and confiscated the guns. However, once their actions were discovered, the brethren were counseled to immediately let the gun runners go peacefully, which they did.

Adam Black

Oh what's to say of Adam Black?
Who pledged to keep the peace
Then stabbed believers in the back
And sought the Saints to fleece

Joseph's View of the Mob
(Gleaned from his own accounts)

Murderous
Oppressive
Blood Thirsty
Old Settlers
Cunning
Rotten Hearted
Angry
Threatening

It was at this same time, that the mob also began to enter the small town of DeWitt in Carroll County, and threaten the Saints there, warning them to leave or be killed. To the north, the militia, called into action by Governor Boggs, actually quelled the mob in Daviess county for a short time and their commander, General Parks, noted the willingness, even eagerness, of the Saints to comply with the law and be protected in their rights. However, as the calm increased in Daviess County, it rapidly deteriorated in Carroll County, and the mob boldly began to fire upon the Saints in DeWitt. It was at these dangerous times, that a large number of Saints from Kirtland arrived in the vicinity of Far West. Those Saints were the people of Kirtland Camp.

Chapter Thirteen

Kirtland Camp

Much of official Church history and other significant writings are filled with reports about Zion's Camp, the famous expedition of Saints, who, with Joseph at their head, left Kirtland with the intention of protecting the Saints in Independence and Clay Counties from the mobs, and perhaps redeeming their lands. Zion's camp, with all of its experiences, miracles, and lessons, is thus very well-known and documented.

Much less known however, is a second major excursion of Saints from Kirtland, who seeking to heed God's call to Zion, moved as a large body from Ohio to establish homes in the Far West region. This camp, known as Kirtland Camp, was organized by the Quorum of the Seventy and during their long journey to Zion they experienced their own miracles and trials. Unlike Zion's Camp, Kirtland Camp was never intended to be a temporary move, or a mere tactical operation. From the beginning the Saints were determined to bind together and move as a body with the intention of settling in and strengthening the new Mormon communities in Daviess and Caldwell Counties. While sadly, the mob actions were to prevent them from that ultimate goal, the lessons they learned and faith they exhibited was not lost. Indeed, many of them would later make the greater, though very similar, exodus from Nauvoo to the Great Salt Lake Valley.

The inspiration for the formation of Kirtland Camp came as the Kirtland Seventies pondered how best to fulfill the Lord's call for the Saints to go up to Zion, and the final decision was surrounded by many spiritual manifestations and witnesses. At the time the faithful brethren in Kirtland, including the Prophet's brother Hyrum Smith, had been working on several strategies to try and assist all of the Saints who felt the need to go up to Zion, to achieve that worthy goal. It was a time of great poverty however, and their plans had all come to naught, to the point that the High Council and the High Priests had decided that if any were to go up, they would have to find the means on their own. Into this depressed and challenging time, the power of the Spirit came, and the Lord provided a revelation to the Presidents of the Seventy:

> ...the spirit of the Lord came down in mighty power, and some of the Elders began to prophesy that if the quorum would go up in a body together, and go according to the commandments and revelations of God, pitching their tents by the way, that they should not want for anything on the journey that would be necessary for them to have; and further that there should be nothing wanting towards removing the whole quorum of the Seventies that would go in a body, but that there should be a sufficiency of all things...[104]

President Foster, one of the seven presidents, then reported to the group that he saw a vision, in which a camp of about five hundred Saints were going up to Zion in an orderly manner. The Holy Spirit so filled the assembly that all present were convinced that it was God's will and so believed that they could and should undertake to do what God had approved. Many of the Elder's Quorum in Kirtland were also caught up in the zeal and sought to join with the Seventies and to move with the camp to Zion.

Let Them Go

> *So solemn scene, when Seventies*
> *With hearts for Zion, met to know*
> *God's will for families looking West*
> *Who longed for Him, to let them go*
>
> *High Priests, High Councils saw no way*
> *To move Saints bound by poverty*
> *Yet Seventies through spirit's light*
> *Beheld God's plan to set them free*
>
> *Alone the hardships were too great*
> *But in one body, strength would come*

> *So Kirtland's Camp, united moved*
> *To Zion, there to find a home*

Once the decision was made and affirmed by so many heavenly manifestations, the excitement of the Saints increased and many more came to believe that it was, in fact, possible to undertake such a thing. One of the first acts of the Seventy was to establish a written constitution or the rules they would follow as a united camp. Interestingly, part of the punishment for those who entered the camp, but then failed to live by the direction of the camp's rules and governing council, was for the offenders to be disfellowshiped from the camp, and "left by the way." The camp constitution for "Kirtland Camp" was agreed to and signed by over a hundred and seventy heads of families.

As the Saints progressed in their planning, the leaders assembled once more in the Kirtland Temple and read the constitution. The spirit of unity and excitement increased. It was at this point that Hyrum Smith, a high priest and one who had labored in the past to find some way to help the Saints migrate to Far West, including looking into chartering a steam boat, came forward and demonstrated his deep humility and meekness. To those assembled Saints, who no doubt knew of his failed attempts to provide a means for them to go, the Prophet's brother and confident, the beloved Hyrum, confessed his weakness. He admitted that all his plans and urging prior to that time with regard to the means by which the Kirtland Saints could move to Zion, had been based upon his own mortal feelings and wisdom, which sometimes God's Saints were left to rely upon. He told the Saints that the failure of his attempts was a witness to him that he had been following his own wisdom and that God had not been behind those plans. The record of the proceedings speaking of Hyrum reports; *"he then declared that he knew by the Spirit of God that the movements that were (sic) making by the quorums of the Seventies for their removal and the plan of their journeying was according to the will of the Lord."*[105]

Hyrum's integrity and humility on this occasion bring to mind the Lord's sweet expression of love for him, when in the Doctrine and

Covenants the Lord tells us that he loves Hyrum, "for the integrity of his heart."[106]

Hyrum's endorsement, along with the other spiritual manifestations, strengthened the Saints and they hastened their preparations. At last on the evening of July 5, 1838, the Kirtland Saints were ready to depart. Though they were not to leave until the next day, one can almost feel the excitement, the faith, even the solemnity that must have filled Kirtland Camp that night. The Church history provides us with this account:

> "The night was clear and the encampment and all around was solemn as eternity; which scene together with the remembrances of those other scenes through which the Saints in Kirtland had passed during the last two years, all presented themselves to the thinking mind; and together with the greatness of the undertaking, the length of the journey and many other things combined, could not fail to awaken sensations that could be better felt than described."[107]

Dawning

Clear summer's night, at dawn we leave
Emotions, memories, flow
Our leader's guidance we believe
By faith, prepared to go

Two trying years, in Kirtland's land
Shall soon become our past
Tomorrow, led by God's great hand
We move to Zion at last

On the morning of 6 July, the Saints that comprised Kirtland Camp left for Zion. Their journey would carry them over hundreds of miles, through storms, through persecutions and threatening, and through discord among some members of the camp. Their journey would be plagued by illnesses and deaths. Yet their undertaking would also be filled with manifestations of the Holy

Spirit, with miraculous healings, with sacrifices and great unity. The majority of the towns and villages through which Kirtland Camp passed, displayed nothing but curiosity and on one occasion, even admiration to see such a large movement of people passing through. One minister even commented on such a sight; "*The movements of the Mormons were actions and not words, and looked more like love and the spirit of union than anything that had come under his observation.*"[108]

There were exceptions however, in that some along the route would profane Church leaders, throw eggs, and even on occasion arrest some of the leaders on charges generally arising from the failure of the Kirtland Safety Society. One particularly Anti-Mormon village even produced a cannon and threatened to fire upon the Saints, but after some consultations between the leaders, they allowed the camp to pass. Through it all, the majority of the Saints remained steadfast and faithful and enjoyed moments of spiritual peace. For example, on the 28th of August, after camping for the night and reviewing the many trials and strugglings they had gone through,

> "The Spirit of God rested down upon the camp with power, and after singing the hymn 'The Spirit of God like a fire is burning,' we concluded by a song 'Hosanna to God and the Lamb,' and retired with joyful hearts to our tents."[109]

As with the Children of Israel, many of the struggles of the Saints came as a result of their own murmurings. However, like Moses' people, the faithful were also blessed with healings and other miraculous preservations. On one occasion the Saints met and offered supplications for the rain to fall. The next day the heavens opened and the drought was broken.

Near the end of their journey, as they approached Far West, the Saints were warned about the many difficulties their brethren in Missouri were facing and were even threatened with that same mob violence. In spite of the threats, the majority pressed forward until on October 2,1838, the Camp having been met a few miles from town by the First Presidency of the Church, made it to Far

West and camped for the night around the foundations of the temple. While for the moment there was great joy for the Saints of Kirtland Camp, it was not to last. Sadly, less than a month after their arrival, Governor Boggs gave his famous extermination order and the Saints began to be driven from such settlements as Dewitt, Adam-Ondi-Ahman, and Far West.

Kirtland Camp

Apostasy and anger, they gladly left behind
Traveling swiftly to Zion, unsure of what they'd find
Trusting in the Lord, their God, They knew to be so kind

Thus journeyed Kirtland Camp

By faith they faced foul weather, cruel hunger and disease
With faith they followed counsel, strove hard their God to please
That faith passing such trials, made stronger by degrees

Thus journeyed Kirtland's Camp

At length their journey ended, the Saints entered Far West
With opened arms were welcomed, on temple ground found rest
Yet then moved to Di'ahman, to fill Joseph's request

Thus Journeyed Kirtland Camp

Zion was then in turmoil, the mobs with Saints at war
And Kirtland Camp's arrival, some courage did restore
Yet mobs who'd fled from Daviess, sought vengeance all the more

Gainst those of Kirtland Camp

Chapter Fourteen

War Upon the Saints

Part One
Abandonment of DeWitt[110]

Soon after the Saints of Kirtland Camp had arrived at Far West and then moved on to help strengthen the Church in the settlement at Adam-Ondi-Ahman, their fellow Saints residing in Dewitt began to face the full fury of the mob. As more and more mobocrats gathered, they began to fire upon the Saints living in Dewitt. At the time Colonel Hinkle had organized the DeWitt Saints into a defense force who, in an attempt to discourage attack through a show of force, returned fire upon the mob. The Missouri militia, with all its bias and poor leadership, had been called out ostensibly to prevent violence, though it was plagued with mob sympathetic militiamen and outright desertions from the militia over to the mob. On October 6th, as soon as the Prophet Joseph received intelligence about the plight of the Saints in Dewitt, he immediately left Far West and headed southeast to join them, and through some careful maneuvering was able to elude the mob members who were guarding the roads and enter Dewitt to join his besieged brethren. In Dewitt, Joseph found to his great sorrow, that the Saints were not only few in number, but almost without food.

At this critical time, the request for help that was dispatched to the governor was denied, Governor Boggs coldly claiming that it was a matter between the Mormons and the mob and that they ought to "fight it out." The Saints' situation was growing worse. If they left town to search for food, they immediately became a target of opportunity for the trigger-happy mob surrounding Dewitt. The situation became so desperate that some of the brethren in Dewitt actually perished from starvation. Recalling those scenes, the Prophet Joseph recorded:

"For once in my life, I had the pain of beholding some of my fellow creatures fall victims to the spirit of persecution, which did then and had since prevailed to such an extent in upper Missouri. They were men too, who were virtuous and against whom no legal process could for one moment be sustained, but who, in consequence of their love of God, attachment to His cause, and their determination to keep the faith, were thus brought to an untimely grave."[111]

Finally, the original (non-Mormon) settlers in DeWitt, brokered a peace agreement that would allow the hopeless Saints to depart in peace, promising that they would repay the Saints for their losses. Trusting in that promise and due to the desperate nature of their situation, the Saints departed. Many of those who lived outside of the town, but who had fled there for safety, discovered on their exodus that their homes had been burned and their cattle killed. Of course, the promise to reimburse the Saints was never fulfilled. Thus, the Saints abandoned Dewitt and moved slowly and painfully toward Far West. Along the two day journey, more of the Saints died from the privations and all they had suffered, including one woman who had just recently given birth and who, due to the circumstances of their flight, was buried in a grove without a coffin. Though not as well-known as others, and sometimes even forgotten, these victims of the cruel mob were none the less martyrs for their faith.

Martyrs of Dewitt

Though virtuous, above reproach
Whom no court could convict
They struggled, victims of the mob
Those martyrs of Dewitt

From homes and living, they were barred
Collected for Defense
No food, no sleep, great toll did take
Death was their recompense

Mrs. Jensen gave birth in Dewitt
From mobs she'd not be saved
They buried her while fleeing west
No coffin for her grave

More Saints would suffer from fatigue
As mob pressed hard behind
Privation stopped their flight too soon
In death, sweet peace, they'd find

Part Two
Defense of Diahman

Not long after the survivors of the retreat from Dewitt had made it to Far West, the tension again began to be focused upon the Saints settled north of Far West, Adam-Ondi-Ahman in particular. The absolute failure of the government to protect the Dewitt Saints emboldened the mob, and greed inspired them with the hope of taking back the lands they had sold to the Saints, thus profiting doubly. The lack of the rule of law opened the door to the vile mob to do whatever they pleased without fear of retribution.

It was at this time that the Prophet Joseph gave a stirring sermon at Far West on the scriptural principle of laying down one's life for his friends, and then asked for volunteers to march with him back into Daviess County to assist in the defense of Adam-Ondi-Ahman. Joseph made it very clear that the volunteers, one hundred strong, who met with him in the public square to begin their march, were officially called up under the laws of the county and were in fact, a militia authorized to restore order. No sooner had Joseph and his forces moved into Diahman, than he witnessed many of the outlaying Saints, whose homes had been burned and livestock run off, fleeing into the settlement for protection from the mob. The prophet thus described the sight,

> Women and children, some in the most delicate condition, where thus obliged to leave their homes and travel several

miles in order to effect their escape. My feelings were such that I cannot describe them when I saw them flock into the village, almost entirely destitute of clothes and only escaping with their lives.[112]

These tragedies did not leave the Prophet's own family untouched. His sister-in-law, Agnes Smith, suffered greatly at the hands of the Daviess County mob, as he records:

> On the evening that General Parks arrived at Diahman, my brother, the late Don Carlos Smith's wife came in to Col. Wight's about eleven o'clock at night, bringing her two children along with her, one about two years and a half old, the other a babe in her arms. She came in on foot, a distance of three miles, and waded Grand River, and the water was then about waist deep, and the snow about 3 inches deep.[113]

Such sacrifices made while her husband was away serving the Lord on a mission, outline the faith and determination, the love and constancy of the Saints of that day.

Agnes Smith

Why risked ye health to bring them forth
How see you in them, endless worth
'Tis mother's love

What kept you whilst Don Carlos served?
How faced you taunts, no soul deserves
Your mother's love

What strengthened you while cabin burned?
Pushed you for miles, whilst your heart yearned
That mother's love

How fled you then with babes through snow
Wade 'cross the Grand's deep icy flow
By mother's love

The impact of seeing all that the Saints were suffering caused Colonel Wight to ask General Parks, his commanding officer, what they could do to stop the mobs, and General Parks told him to order out his men of the 59th regiment. As the regiment formed with the express intention of dispersing the mob or to die in the attempt, the mobs discovered their coming, knew of their determination, and so they fled, at least for a time. [114]

Wight's 59th

Come boys, we've heard the widow's cry
No nobler cause in which to die

To fight to free our faith's oppressed
Put down the mobs, bring Saints sweet rest

Though we be few, we will not fear
Like Saints of old, our duty's clear

With Colonel Wight to lead us on
We'll not stay hands, 'til mobs are gone

And should we die, in this defense
We'll trust our God's sweet recompense

****

> *Rest now my boys for mobs have fled*
> *Our courage, filled their hearts with dread*
>
> *They'd not, the back bone, for the fight*
> *'Gainst our cause that they knew was right*
>
> *Yet, since with greed their hearts still burn*
> *In greater numbers they'll return*

While this temporary retreat of the mob gave some encouragement to the Saints, it was not long before the mob employed a strategy to increase their own numbers. They began to empty and then burn some of their own selected homes, and then blame the actions on the Mormons to incite public opinion against the Saints to an even greater extent. In the short reprieve provided by the mob's retreat, the Prophet Joseph Smith returned to Far West from Daviess County in company of some brethren who had served with him there in support of the Saints. His hope was that the Saints might "enjoy some respite," but it was not to be. The actions of the mob in continuing its false claims had angered the citizenry and inspired other mobs, who in turn, were attacking the Saints on the borders of Caldwell County. Saints from those areas were gathering in large numbers to Far West to escape the depredations of the mob.

At that point, the Saints in Far West who were preparing their defenses, discovered a cannon the mob had brought in from Independence, which was buried for future use against them. Upon discovering the cannon, the Saints confiscated it. However, the mob turned that setback to their advantage claiming that the Mormons were using that cannon in their attacks upon the people of Missouri. In such perilous and trying times, as the Saints were constantly being accused falsely from without, the apostasy and flight of Thomas Marsh, who was supported in part by Orson Hyde, only served to fuel the already intense fire of Anti-Mormon sentiment. Most damaging were the Danite allegations already mentioned. Increasingly, the tensions, panic and near chaos among both the mob and Saints set the stage for the tragic, and yet heroic battle of Crooked River.[115]

Part Three
The Battle of Crooked River[116]

In late October of 1838, a mob under the leadership of a Mr. Bogart had begun to threaten the outlying Mormon homes in Caldwell County. They would enter the homes and order the Saints to leave under threat of death. One of the brethren thus threatened sent word to Far West to inform them of what was happening and then took it upon himself to watch the movements of the mob. Other Saints left Far West, with the intent to keep watch on the mob and while in that service, witnessed the mob taking three Mormon prisoners, Nathan Pinkham, William Seely and Addison Green. It was reported that the mob intended to kill their prisoners that night. In response to that intelligence, Colonel Hinkle ordered out the Far West militia to disperse the mob and save the prisoners. At midnight on the square in Far West, seventy-five Latter-day Saints volunteered to go with the Apostle David W. Patten at their head. Their mission was to attempt to scare off the mob and retrieve the prisoners. With that intent, the force immediately set out to find the mobbers' camp. Near dawn on the morning of the 25th of October, the main body of the Mormon forces dismounted near the ford on the Crooked River which lies just south of the Caldwell County line, and began a foot march in search of the mob's camp with its prisoners.[117]

As the Far West militia passed over the crown of the hill on the road leading to the river, they heard a single shot and one of their own, Patrick O'Bannion, fell mortally wounded. That was the start of the skirmish that has since been called the Battle of Crooked River. The Saints were at a disadvantage in that they were firing into the dark, while the dawn, arising at their backs, allowed their silhouettes to be observed by the mob. Several volleys were exchanged in which a few more of the Saints were hit. As the Saints returned fire, they yelled, "God and Liberty" and then at the command of Captain Patten, charged into the mob with their muskets and swords. The hand to hand combat was intense, but short lived, and the mob fled leaving behind their prisoners and several wounded brethren. Tragically, as one of the mob members was fleeing, he turned and shot Captain Patten, mortally wounding him in the bowels. After the skirmish, the brethren rounded up the wounded and dead, collected the freed prisoners, and carried them back toward Far West.

While in one sense the battle was successful, in that both the mission to free the prisoners and that to disperse the mob were completed, it also came at a great cost to the lives and health of the valiant and faithful Mormon militiamen from Far West. It also exacted a future toll upon the Saints. No sooner had the skirmish ended than the rumors, lies and embellished reports began to circulate throughout Missouri, with the eventual result of creating an even larger ground swell of public opinion against the Saints, and subsequently the raising of another state sponsored, though mob supplied, militia to put down the "Mormon Rebellion". Thus, the Battle of Crooked River revealed both the best and worst of mankind. It displayed the penchant of humans to believe anything that is calculated to incite anger, and who will then stop at nothing to impose their faith and beliefs, or exercise their bigotry upon others or even simply to persecute those who are different. In that essence, the battle and subsequent destruction of the entire community at Far West, were in one very sad way, a form of an American Holocaust. Those events help to answer the question, "Could a holocaust ever happen in the land of the free?" Yes, it could, and it has. On the other hand, the battle revealed the heroism, valor and faith of the Saints, who willingly risked all they had in the cause of their God, willingly given in defense of their faith and their fellow brethren. Indeed, the war cry of that small Far West militia, as it sounded on the banks of the Crooked River that October morning, outlines in exactness what was truly to be found in the hearts of the Saints on that fateful day, a sincere devotion to "God and Liberty."

**<u>Battle of Crooked River
A Ballad</u>**

They met upon the square, hunched 'gainst the chilly air
Each felt there was to be a mighty fight
"Boys set aside your fears", "for we need volunteers"
"To move against the mob this very night!"

"The mob has captured three", "and we must set them free"
"Or they'll not see the light of this next day"
"Delays we can't afford", "thus trusting in our Lord"
"We call for volunteers, what do you say?"

Each man's heart leapt to hear, each pushed against the fear
Young Patrick moved and said; "well, count me in"
Men's gazes left the ground, to hear such courage sound
Soon seventy were ready to begin

Dave Patten took the lead, mounted his anxious steed
And led his men towards Crooked River's ford
Determined not to fail, They'd scour every vale
Then free their captive brothers with the sword!

They searched 'til nearly dawn, determined to press on
Dismounted when the mobbers' camp they found
Just yards from their intent, the morning air was rent
One musket shot knocked Patrick to the ground

The mob was now in range, so vollies they'd exchange
The sun behind the brethren marked them well
The balls flew thick as flies, pierced stomachs, arms and thighs
"For God and Liberty" each Saint did yell

When Patten gave the word, with musket and with sword,
The brethren charged downhill toward hellish band
Then volunteers drew nigh, and with a mighty cry
Engaged the mob in fighting hand to hand

Then mob, the Saints did best, struck fear in all the rest
And soon the mob broke free, in panic fled
Yet as the fiends did flee, one fired from a tree
Shot Elder Patten, leaving him for dead

With battle all but won, the mob well on the run
The brethren freed the captives who'd survived
The wounded gathered in, the long march did begin
The full cost they'd not know till they arrived

Some brethren's wounds would heal, others the wounds would kill
Among them Carter, Patrick, Patten too
They met a martyr's fate, victims of cruel hate
Yet to their God and faith, they had been true

Chapter Fifteen

David W. Patten: Apostle & Martyr

While Elder Patten survived the Battle of Crooked River for a short time, and was still alive as the militia headed back toward Far West, the traveling caused him such great pain, that at length, they stopped at a Brother Winchester's house about three miles from Far West. Hearing of the news of the battle, the Prophet Joseph, Hyrum his brother, and Lyman Wight, left Far West to meet the returning warriors and then in great sorrow, witnessed the distress of their beloved friends, in particular the apostle Elder David W. Patten, who was suffering at the point of death.

Elder Patten was baptized into the Church June 15, 1832, in Indiana and immediately set about to preach the restored gospel. He was a valiant missionary and often used his gift of healing, acting as a tool of God in restoring health to those he taught. He worked many miracles and demonstrated many other gifts of the spirit throughout his life. In 1834, David felt led to join the Saints in Zion which he did, joining up with them in Clay County. David was also one of the original Twelve Apostles, being called in February of 1835. He spent his life in service to the Church serving many missions and defying mobs in Tennessee and Kentucky. He became well known for his courage and spirited defenses of his faith, to the end that he was even known by some members of the Church by the appellation, "Captain Fear Not"[118] Elder Patten eventually returned to Missouri to join the Saints in Far West in September of 1836, where he stayed until his death in 1838, occasioned by the battle of Crooked River.[119]

Elder Patten is mentioned by the Lord in the Doctrine and Covenants and markedly so. In Section 124, the Lord twice mentions Elder Patten. In verse 19, the Lord declares that David Patten is with him at the time of the revelation, and in company with Edward Partridge and Joseph Smith Senior, who had also passed away. Then again in verse 130, the Lord affirms that he has taken Elder Patten unto himself, and adds that his priesthood,

"No man taketh from him..."[120] Given those revelations concerning Elder Patten, it can be said with confidence, "It is well with his soul."

Of the final scenes of Elder Patten's life, Heber C. Kimball records:

> Although he had medical assistance, yet his wound was such, that there was no hope entertained of his recovery: this he was perfectly aware of. In this situation while the shades of time were lowering, and eternity with all its realities was opening to his view, he bore a strong testimony to the truth of the work of the Lord, and the religion he had espoused.
>
> He all the while expressed a great desire to depart. I spoke to him and said, "Brother David, when you get home, I want you to remember me." He exclaimed, "I will."
>
> At this time his sight was gone. We felt so very much attached to our beloved brother, that we beseeched the Lord to spare his life and endeavored to exercise faith for his recovery. Of this he was perfectly aware, and expressed a desire that we should let him go, as his desire was to be with Christ, which was far better.
>
> A few minutes before he died, he prayed as follows: Father, I ask thee, in the name of Jesus Christ, that thousand (sic) wouldst release my spirit and receive it unto thyself:" and then said to those who surrounded his dying bed, "Brethren you have held me by your faith, but do give (sic) me up and let me go I beseech you." We committed him to God, and he soon breathed his last, and slept in Jesus without a groan. [121]

Thus, were the winding up scenes of the first apostle of this dispensation, to give up his life and die a martyr for the cause. That he was faithful to the end is revealed in the interesting and beautiful message contained in Elder Patten's last comments, made to his wife to whom he said; "Whatever you do else, O do not deny the faith."[122]

Just before the funeral, as the Prophet Joseph walked into Elder Patten's home and beheld the scene of the mourners around the body of Elder Patten, he was moved upon to cry; *"There lies the man that has done just as he said he would-he has laid down his life for his friends"*[123] Later, in his journal, the Prophet Joseph wrote a befitting epitaph for Elder Patten:

> *"Brother David Patten was a very worthy man, beloved by all good men who knew him. He was one of the Twelve Apostles, and died as he had lived, a man of God, and strong in the faith of a glorious resurrection, in a world were mobs will have no power or place.*[124]

<u>Elder David Patten</u>
<u>A Sonnet</u>

Among the first modern apostles named
This valiant son of God, who feared no man
Who healed the sick, and evil spirits tamed
Winnowed the wheat and chaff, with faith's great fan

Interpreter of tongues by holy gift
Survivor of grave threats upon his life
He did from death bed's feeble suffers lift
And comfort brought to Far West Saints in strife

With courage led the charge at crooked Creek
Shot down by angry mob, then in retreat
At death his wife's own welfare he did seek
Encouragement to faithfulness repeat

The Lord has claimed dear David as his own
No man shall take his priesthood, nor his crown

Chapter Sixteen

Siege of Far West

With the death of Elder Patten, and in light of the rumors surrounding the Battle of Crooked River, the anger and boldness of the mob did increase and thus strengthened by many volunteers from the surrounding counties, the mob prepared to exercise their unrestrained revenge upon the hated Mormons. Even worse for the Saints, the mobs had formed up into militias, under the color of state law, and were led by mob generals, with the Governor's authority. Just two days after the battle of Crooked River, Governor Boggs, a victim of his own hatred and prejudice, issued the infamous extermination order. In a communiqué to his military leaders Governor Boggs wrote "...The Mormons must be treated as enemies and must be exterminated or driven from the state..."[125] That any governmental decree calling for the extermination of a people could be issued within the constitutional protections of the United States is almost unbelievable, yet many years after that order was issued, the world witnessed scenes from Germany and Russia which teach us again that such inhumanity, is in fact, within the hearts of evil men of all nations.

The Order

Based on reports I've heard of late
About those Mormons whom I hate
I order them to leave the state
And those who stay...exterminate!

The effect of the extermination order was powerful upon the enemies of the Saints as the militias continued to increase in size and the mobs lost any fear of retribution. The first to suffer the full extent of the mob's religious hatred, unbridled by human decency or rule of law, were the Saints gathered at a small settlement near Far West on the banks of Shoal Creek. Just three days after the issuance of the extermination order the mob exercised its fury and attacked Hawn's Mill.

In the afternoon, a mob about three hundred strong, surrounded the tiny Hawn's Mill settlement. They ignored all pleas for quarters, and began to cruelly murder those who pled for mercy. A small group of armed Saints fled to a blacksmith shop where they began to fire back at the mob in self defense. The mob, enjoying their vastly superior numbers, surrounded the structure and continued to pour volley after volley of fire into it, until all of the small defending band were killed or wounded. In the heat of the attack, the mob did not spare children, killing some and wounding others. At length, as the terror subsided, the attackers then ransacked the settlement and threatened the survivors with death if they did not leave. In all, seventeen Saints were killed including two children. Another twelve or thirteen were wounded including one child and one young woman.[126]

Hawn's Mill

The work of death..those words describe it best
That awful day at Hawn's Mill, near Far West

Why were we there? Joseph asked us to leave
Mobs shoot us down? We just could not believe

But oh what dread, to see that mob appear
Three hundred strong, their vile intent was clear

Men sued for peace, as women ran to hide
But heeding not, they cut down Tom McBride

'Gainst such great odds, our men their doom could sense
In blacksmith shop, they formed their weak defense

A moment's pause, then mobs upon them broke
The air was filled, with musket balls and smoke

Soon all were down, some wounded some were dead
Mob howled like fiends, ransacked our homes, then fled

The Sun had set, before we chanced again
To see Hawn's Mill, our murdered boys and men

Oh awful night, our own howls filled the air
At loss so deep, hearts torn with deep despair

How can it be, that evil should so reign
In hearts of men, who caused such cruel pain

But still we know, that justice will be done
When mobs must stand, before the Holy One

What awful day, when each upon their knees
Account for deeds, done to the "least of these"

The same day of the Hawn's Mill Massacre, the state militia who had failed in their pretended mission to protect the innocent at Hawn's Mill, were busy threatening the Saints at Far West. They marched to within view of the town, then seeing the defenses, marched a mile away and encamped for the night. The next day the vastly outnumbered Far West defenders continued to throw up makeshift fortifications and the women gathered their belongings, fearing their homes would be burned. At that point, the mob militia sent a flag of truce to the encircled town, and Colonel Hinkle, who had command of the Mormon defenders, spoke privately with the party that carried the flag. The unforeseen circumstance of a possible truce filled the Saints with hope that some resolution could be reached to stop the inevitable battle. During the negotiations with Colonel Hinkle, he agreed to all of the militia's terms, which included the surrendering of Joseph and other Church leaders to the mob, surrendering the weapons of the Far West defenders, a promise by the Saints to repay all damages, and a commitment to leave the state by the next spring.

Subsequently, Colonel Hinkle met with the Prophet and told him that the militia leaders wanted to speak with him and others about some way to peacefully resolve the situation. Instead of negotiations however, as soon as the church leaders were in the militia's clutches, they were arrested as prisoners of war and treated with contempt and ridicule. The next day, Thursday, 1 November, Joseph, Hyrum and others were tried by court martial and sentenced to be shot in the Far West town square on Friday morning. That sentence was never carried out, thanks in a large part, to the courageous stance of General Doniphan, who responded to General Lucas' execution orders as follows "*It is cold blooded murder, I will not obey your order. My brigade shall march for Liberty tomorrow morning at 8 o'clock, and if you execute these men, I will hold you accountable before an earthly tribunal, so help me God.*"[127]

General Doniphan's courage spared Joseph and his brethren from execution, but they remained in custody of the mob militia, and eventually were deposited in Liberty Jail, where they were to suffer for many months. At this same time, since it was Colonel Hinkle who had made his private agreement with the mob, he in turn, ordered his men to stand down, and a part of the mob militia was given free reign over the people and buildings in Far West. Thus, being free, they plundered the homes, and abused the inhabitants dreadfully. Later Colonel Hinkle's Caldwell militia were forced to give up their personal arms, and the militia under General Lucas, once again committed many acts of depravity against the unarmed Saints remaining in Far West.

On Friday Morning, rather than being executed, Joseph and the brethren were marched into Far West and allowed to bid their families farewell. That act was not so much one of mercy, as it was a deliberate taunting of the Mormon faithful. The heart wrenching scenes of that bitter farewell, as recorded by the Prophet Joseph, not only highlight the sacrifices those faithful Far West Saints made for their faith, but adds new meaning to Section 122 of the Doctrine and Covenants. That powerful section, given to the Prophet Joseph Smith as he languished in Liberty Jail and in response to his pleadings, suddenly becomes more real and powerful with the realization that the Lord was not just making up likely scenarios of the tragedies that might befall the Prophet, but rather was recounting to the Prophet in livid detail, the tragedies he had already gone through at Far West. It was as if the Lord were proving to the Prophet, that on that cold morning in

November 1838, the Lord was neither absent nor unconcerned, but was in fact, standing with Joseph as those scenes unfolded. The Lord said in part,

> "...if thine enemies fall upon thee; if they tear thee from the society of thy father and mother and brethren and sisters; and if with a drawn sword thine enemies tear thee from the bosom of thy wife, and of thine offspring, and thine elder son, although but six years of age, shall cling to thy garments, and shall say, My father, my father, why can't you stay with us? O, my father, what are the men going to do with you? and if then he shall be thrust from thee by the sword..."[128]

Think of the comfort such a personal recounting, direct from Heavenly Father, would bring; imagine the powerful significance it would have to the Prophet who, of those same events in Far West, wrote:

> "who can realize the feelings which I experienced at that time, to be thus torn from my companion, and leave her surrounded by monsters in the shape of men, and my children too, not knowing how their wants would be supplied; while I was to be taken far from them in order that my enemies might destroy me when they thought proper to do so. My partner wept, my children clung to me, until they were thrust from me by the swords of the guards..."[129]

Lyman Wight, in a later affidavit about the Missouri persecutions, described part of those same scenes in these words:

> "...his eldest son Joseph, about six or eight years old, hanging to the tail of his coat, crying 'Father is the mob going to kill you?' The guard said to him, 'You d-- little brat, go back; you will see your father no more'"[130]

Thus, the historical record makes it clear that the true answer to the Prophet's rhetorical question as to whether God was aware of all he had suffered, is yes! His Father in Heaven could and did realize all that he had gone through on that bitter morning. He knew it all in perfect detail. What a powerful answer for the burdened prophet who began his imprisoned inquiry with the words, "O God, where art thou? And where is the pavilion that covereth thy hiding place?"[131]

Where Art Thou

Where art Thou God, where cans't Thou be?
Why wil'st Thou not, our troubles see?
Why must Thy servants suffer so?
Wil'st Thou on them some mercy show?

My son let thy soul be at peace
My love and mercy never cease
I've seen it all, from first to last
Thou offerest me all that thou hast

Like Abraham, you've not held back
And now your offerings, nothing lack
You're consecrated, sanctified
Cleansed from the willfulness of pride

Each of your sufferings I do know
And each, your faith, has helped to grow
Each I've descended far below

Art thou greater than me?

All that I have shall yours now be
Through time and all eternity

After being torn away from their families, the prisoners were moved to Richmond Jail, where the famous rebuking of the guards took place, and then on to Liberty Jail. During that time, General Clark, after securing more prisoners among the brethren still at Far West, addressed the remaining Saints, falsely laying the fault for their suffering upon their own heads, and then prophesying with all the accuracy of a priest of Baal: " *As for your leaders, do not once think-do not imagine for a moment-do not let it enter your mind that they will be delivered, or that you will see their faces again, for their fate is fixed-their die is cast-their doom is sealed.*"[132] Of course, General Clark was in error, and more than just in his lack of ability to correctly see the future.

After thus attempting to harangue the Saints in Far West, General Clark sent a portion of the militia to Adam-Ondi-Ahman to arrest and detain many more members, all of which were later acquitted. As part of those movements, the Saints in Adam-Ondi-Ahman were ordered from their homes and given the choice of going to Far West to await the spring, when they would then be forced to leave the state, or to just pack up and leave the state immediately. Thus, Far West became a sort of internment camp, to hold the Saints until they would leave the state. The mob militia did allow a committee of the brethren from Far West to travel to Adam-Ondi-Ahman to collect what was left of their belongings. It was amidst this persecution, with many of their leaders still in the hands of the enemy, and the Saints in Missouri suffering greatly, that the High Council, composed of those faithful brethren remaining in Far West met on December 13th.

At that sacred meeting, President Brigham Young arose, called for the Saints to use order and caution in their dealings, and then, in the face of such terrible oppression as they had suffered, reaffirmed his own faith. While some of the Saints were questioning their cause, and others had left their fellowship and turned from the faith, Brigham Young stood boldly and reaffirmed his faith in the Gospel of Jesus Christ, to the gathered council. His example was then followed by Heber C Kimball and the rest of the council, who in turn, testified as to their faith in Joseph Smith as a prophet, in the Book of Mormon and other aspects of the restored gospel, some even claimed that the recent trials had made their faith stronger. What a powerful meeting that must have been, as they met in their humbled circumstances, soon to be homeless, and yet did not doubt, but remained filled with faith.[133]

December Council

(Based on their actual statements of faith)

Brigham Young:

It's true by mobs we've suffered much
    Our leaders languish in their clutch
        And many's faith has failed for such
    Yet mine's as strong as ever

Heber C. Kimball:

I've tried to live, to not offend
    What I've done wrong, I'll strive to mend
        And to my duty, I'll attend
    My faith's as strong as ever

Simeon Carter:

This Church is by a prophet led
    None will be planted in his stead
        I'll live so glory crowns my head
    I trust Joseph as ever

Jared Carter:

I'm pleased to hear each brother talk
In fellowship with you I'll walk

Thomas Grover:

My faith is firm, which such hope brings
Joseph will one day stand with kings

David Dort:

Though not well known in deeds or name
My faith and feelings are the same!

Levi Jackman:

I know not what awaits us hence
In Joseph, I've still confidence

Solomon Hancock:

In modern scripture I believe
   Joseph as prophet I receive
       God, Joseph's burdens shall relieve
   And raise him up on high

John Badger:

Our scourges teach us all the more
My faith is stronger than before

George W. Harris:

In thorny paths that we have trod
I see the mighty hand of God

Samuel Bent:

My faith these scourges did not phase
In pris'n or dungeon, God I'll praise

Three days after that revealing council meeting, the Prophet Joseph from his captivity in Liberty jail, composed an open letter to the Saints in Caldwell County and to those scattered abroad. The letter, which is rich with concern and prophetic love for the faithful Saints and all they had suffered, compared the actions of the militia and mob with those of Haman from the Old Testament, who persecuted and sought the destruction of the Jews.[134]

Joseph also used the letter to denounce all those who apostatized or turned against the Church throughout the Missouri persecutions, and then specifically denied all the false rumors which had been rampantly spread about the Church and its leaders. Those foul rumors had included allegations of Saints burning the homes of non-members, innuendo that the Saints were practicing a community of wives, allegations of the Prophet's approval of the evil practices and secret combinations of Dr. Avard and others, and claims of murder and adultery. Joseph referred to all who claimed that such misconduct could be found among the faithful in the Church as liars. Finally, the Prophet encouraged the Saints to keep faithful and then, like Peter of old, Joseph even gloried in the persecutions they had suffered; *"We glory in our tribulation, because we know that God is with us, that He is our friend, and that He will save our souls. We do not care for them that kill the body, they cannot harm our souls."*[135]

Thus we see, that even though the end of the Saint's settlement at Far West and in other parts of Caldwell County was soon to come, both the Saints who still dwelt there under persecution, and their leaders who languished in Liberty Jail, shared a common resolution to remain faithful to the end. That faith comes to us today as another powerful lesson from Far West.

Chapter Seventeen

Covenant Committee

A little over a month after the Prophet's letter was composed, the Saints in Far West met again in two significant public meetings with the express purpose of finding a way to comply with the unlawful, yet still compelling orders of Governor Boggs, and to facilitate the removal of all the Saints from the state. The meeting was called to order by Don Carlos Smith, the Prophet's brother, and the topic of the first meeting was how the Saints could possibly comply with the Governor's demands given their devastating poverty. It was soon resolved that a committee should be formed to investigate the actual needs of the Saints, to draft a plan or proposal for their removal and to solicit help from both members and citizens of northern Missouri alike, to accomplish the task. While the meeting was listed as public, and not a High Council meeting, it is interesting to note the powerful personalities who made up that first committee of seven, namely: John Taylor, Alanson Ripley, Brigham Young, Theodore Turley, Heber C. Kimball, John Smith, and Don Carlos Smith.

The committee met again just three days later, in which John Taylor presented to the group a memorial of all the persecutions and wrongs the Saints had suffered at the hands of the mobs and politicians while in Missouri, and directed that the document be finished and circulated to the press. At this point Brigham Young, always attuned to the needs of the poor, made a motion that those present would covenant to stand by the poor and needy and assist them with removing from Missouri and escaping the extermination order. The body of those Saints who had gathered agreed and further appointed seven brethren to direct that process for the poor. Consistent with that covenant and the intention of all present, the body drafted a written covenant and subscribed to it on January 29, 1839, in Far West. That beautiful covenant, in sweet harmony with the Lord's command to always remember the poor, read in part:

"We, whose names are hereunder written, do for ourselves individually hereby covenant to stand by and assist one another, to the utmost of our abilities, in removing from this state in compliance with the authority of the state...till there shall not be one left who desires to remove from the state..."[136]

In total, three hundred and eighty Latter-day Saints subscribed to the covenant. Among the signers where members that would yet play important roles in the history of the Church, such as: Brigham Young, George A. Smith, Anson Call, John Taylor, Heber C. Kimball, Don Carlos Smith, Nathan Night, John D. Lee, Stephen Markham, Levi Hancock, and Orin P. Rockwell.

The Covenant

All we who in faith, this covenant subscribe
Do promise that we, for our poor will care
All that we do have, all that still remains
with those who have not, in Christ's name we'll share

The governor's mobs, empowered by writ
Our Saints who remain, will exterminate
Thus all must have means, not one will be left
All who still be Saints, must now leave the state

By council select, this plan will go forth
In wisdom each Saint, will sell off their lands
United in faith, we'll lift up the poor
And thus then fulfill, what our God commands

The original committee selected a new, sort of sub-committee, with the specific focus of removing the Saints from Far West. That committee consisted of eleven members, namely: William Huntington, Charles Bird, Alanson Ripley, Theodore Turley, Daniel Shearer, Shadrach Roundy, Jonathan Hale, Elias Smith, Erastus Bingham, Stephen Markham, and James Newberry. During February 1839, the removal committee also resolved to set priorities as to who would first be assisted in leaving. They determined that the families of the still imprisoned Church leaders should have first priority. Subsequently, and pursuant to that decision, Stephen Markham personally assisted Emma Smith and her children to Illinois, afterward returning immediately to Far West to continue with his committee duties. The committee worked hard on their purpose through February 1839, seeking food and other support and helping the poor and destitute families to leave Missouri. The majority of the exiled Saints being removed from Far West, were moved to the area of Quincy, Illinois, until land in the area of Commerce (Nauvoo) was purchased. During February, the mob persecution of the Far West Saints intensified to the degree that Brigham Young was forced to leave Missouri and flee to Illinois. Additionally, near the later end of February, some of the committee spent some time in Liberty trying all in their power to obtain the release of Joseph and his fellow prisoners, but were unsuccessful and so returned to Far West.[137]

In March, the committee voted to "remember" those who had subscribed to help the poor, but who had then done nothing toward that promise. They further resolved to continue to seek assistance from any Saints who still had means. Additionally, the Prophet Joseph had authorized the Saints to sell their holy lands, and the committee made that known to the remaining Saints, a fact which no doubt, devastated them.[138] Thus began the last stage of the exodus from Far West. Of note, Parley P. Pratt's wife, who had been staying near him while he was at Liberty Jail, left Liberty and joined the Saints in Far West at that time in order to obtain passage to Illinois.

While working with all the issues that the removal of the Saints from Missouri entailed, the committee also worked on issues for the Prophet and his fellow prisoners, including seeing to their personal needs, and presenting their petitions to the state government in Jefferson City. On one such mission in early April, Brothers Turley and Kimball spoke with Joseph through the prison bars, and were encouraged by Joseph's prophecy that the prisoners would soon be delivered, but only by God's hand. Joseph, in turn, warned them to get the Saints out of Missouri as soon as possible.

Service on the committee was wrought with danger. Stephen Markham, in one of his visits to his imprisoned prophet, was told by the Prophet to leave very early in the morning with the promise that if he did, he would escape death at the hands of the mob. He complied and left for Far West very early, contrary to his original plan, and thus escaped the mob who had intended to kill him and who for a time, sought to find him. [139]

Another member of the mentioned committee, Elder Turley, was also often threatened with destruction at the hands of the mob. In mid-April, while conducting business of the committee, a mob of twelve riders approached his home expressing the intent to shoot him. They vandalized his home, breaking furniture and windows. At one point, they even shot down some cows that his daughters were milking. Thankfully, the only harm that came to Brother Turley, was from an Iron pot that the mob hit him with. That same mob which threatened to "*put daylight through*" the committee, had earlier in the day threatened to kill Heber C. Kimball, who, knowing the danger, none the less, boldly informed them that he was indeed a Mormon. That day many of the Saints' homes were ransacked and plundered for anything of value, as the remaining faithful collected what they could and fled.[140]

As a whole, the removal committee at Far West functioned excellently and with the aid of heaven, accomplished their missions. Their dedication of all they had, (even when their own families were also suffering greatly), and their pointed determination to assist the poor and carry out their labors, even at the threat of death, is a wonderful example of how Zion ought to be. Such efforts no doubt, gave experience and wisdom to those involved in that labor, which would inform other future such projects like the Perpetual Emigration Fund. Their true faith and valiant lives were in stark contrast to the motivations behind a very different committee working in the area at that same time. The Vigilance Committee, established by the mob with the purpose of ridding the state of Mormons, was simultaneously engaged in their vile work, which hastened the death of Far West.

Chapter Eighteen

Death of a City

With the mob continuing their pressure, and the Saints fleeing the state as soon as they were able, it was not long until what was once the largest city in Caldwell County, and which served as its county seat, was dead. An obviously biased, yet still informative newspaper article about the final days of Far West records:

> About the period of the final expulsion of the Mormons an association was instituted which might be termed a Vigilance Committee. These made it their business to compel the removal of all persons who were suspected of being in sympathy with these obnoxious fanatics, and for many months during the winter of 1839-40, mob law was supreme in Caldwell county.[141]

It was at the same time in which the Vigilance Committee was working, that Brother Turley had his remarkable encounter with the mob, as already expounded in Chapter Eight, in which he stood firm in support of the revelations of Doctrine and Covenants, Section 118, and boldly testified to his faithfulness to the Prophet in the face of the mob's ridicule.

The Prophet's own history does not record much about the last days of Far West, as his focus had moved to Commerce, Quincy, petitions to the government for redress, and his escape from his illegal imprisonment. However, he does make one sad and final note under the date of Saturday, April 20, where he simply records: *"The last of the Saints left Far West"*[142]

For the rest of the story, as to why all that remains today of a city that once housed thousands, is the temple lot with the cornerstones, we turn to the explanation found in that same newspaper article which earlier described the Vigilance Committee:

Emigrants from all parts of the Union flocked into the county with bitter hatred in their hearts towards Mormonism and everything pertaining to it. The very name of Far West was an abominable sound in the ears of settlers; and after holding courts for about two and a half years longer, in the place, the county seat was removed to a locality called in honor of Austin A. King, Kingston, and which remains today the capital of Caldwell County. In the same year, the Post Office, the first ever established in the limits of the county, which had been held by David Hughes for three years, was removed from Far West to the new county seat. Many who had obtained lawful possession of the buildings in the old town, moved them away, but a large portion of these deserted habitations were carried off, piecemeal by parties who had no shadow of claim to their possession, or were wantonly destroyed by others with whom the vandal spirit of destruction was paramount to every just claim; and in a very few years from the period of the expulsion of the Mormons, scarcely a vestige remained of the once populous and flourishing town of Far West. [143]

It should be noted that this article was written in 1875, only thirty-five years after the expulsion of the Saints. Since it is now over one hundred and seventy years since Far West was abandoned, it is not hard to understand how the rest of those few scarce vestiges could also disappear. However, though the vestiges are gone, the heritage, sacrifices, and service of its one time inhabitants still linger.

Far West: A Hymn

(To the tune of If You Could Hie to Kolob)

On the plains near Olaha Shinehah
Where Adam walked the earth
God sanctified the land where
Far West would have its birth

A holy place to gather
Where Zion's, Saints would see
A refuge from earth's trials
Where God would make them free

Saints came from Independence
Chased north by hate's foul hand
Saints fled from Kirtland's darkness
Sought peace on Holy land

There for one shining moment
sweet peace their souls enjoyed
'til by sin and oppression
Their Zion was destroyed

Now Far West's but a memory
Homes gone and Saints are fled
Now fields and farms conceal their
Foundations and their dead

Yet those with Heavenly vision
Far West may still perceive
Where Saints and stones wait ready
Their temples to receive

Chapter Nineteen

Still There

As sad as it is to ponder on the now empty land where once a city thrived, the truth is, that the land was, in fact, indelibly changed by its one time inhabitants in two very significant ways that cannot be dimmed by time. In fact, in the author's opinion, those changes form the reason why the Holy Spirit still lingers at Far West and touches the hearts of all who visit its holy grounds.

First, the land of Far West is still the burial site of many of the Saints who lived and died there, including the apostle, Elder David W. Patten. While the exact location of the Far West Burial Ground is not known today, and there are no doubt, many other Saints buried in various other places in the outskirts of that holy land, the Far West Historical Society has undertaken to find and preserve that burial ground. Their website provides a compiled list of those known to be, or in some cases believed to be, buried on those sacred grounds. They have made plans to erect a marker in the approximate location of the cemetery in order to honor the dead, most of whom were faithful Saints. Thus, Far West and its environs, still house the remains of those who await the glorious resurrection and whose presence cannot be removed by time, the weather, vandals or any act of man.

Some of those faithful Saints still buried there are: David Patten, the great apostle, and one of the first members of the Quorum of the Twelve and Patrick O'Bannion the first casualty of the battle of Crooked River. Swain Williams, the 19 year old son of Frederick G. Williams, is interred in those grounds, which also house the mortal tabernacle of Amoranda Murdock, wife of John Murdock, a prominent Elder in the Church at Far West, and in later Church history. Loranne, the wife of Elder John E. Page, who was called to the apostleship at Far West, as well as two of the Page children are also buried there. Lyman Sherman is there, who, though not well known, was in the first High Council after the Prophet Joseph's arrest, but who died a little over a month later. James

Marsh, the son of Thomas B. Marsh, who had a remarkable vision as a nine year old boy, is also buried at Far West. The holy and sacred nature of James Marsh's experiences, including his vision of God, were reflected upon soon after his burial in the form of a tribute and a poem which appeared in the last volume of the Far West edition of the Elder's Journal. The poem follows:

Thus ends the life of this dear youth,
Who loved the way that leads to heaven.
In wisdom's paths he sought the truth,
His manners mile, (sic) his temper even.

In vision bright he soared above
And saw the Father face to face,
He heard the angels sing God's love,
And saw his own abiding place.
He talked with Christ, and saw his name,
Within the Book of Life inscribed.
He's gone to realize the same,
With God and angels to abide.[144]

These are just a few of those whose mortal tabernacles lie at Far West awaiting the glorious resurrection. There are many others who lie buried there, including fourteen children.

Truly the interment of so many martyrs and faithful servants of God, render that quiet and empty farm land which was once Far West, a hallowed and sacred place. Yet there is one other aspect of Far West, which also contributes greatly to its sacredness. That is that while all other remnants of civilization seem to have been swept off, the temple site, dedicated and approved by God, with its cornerstones still in place, has survived. In fact, in 1880, three LDS missionaries passing through the Far West area found the temple site, lingered there, and recorded their feelings:

> *"We sat upon the cornerstone reflecting upon the scenes which took place on that memorable day. Following that, it was moved, seconded and carried unanimously by all present (the number being three Elders from Zion) that we*

> *continue to importune at the throne of grace that the Lord will remember the waste places of Zion and permit his Saints to erect the contemplated Temple at Far West in the near future, and also enable them to build a city and organize a Stake of Zion there."*[145]

Those who visit the site today, which sits within the boundaries of the Far West Stake of Zion, with very little effort can imagine a future time, when a small, yet extremely significant temple, begun over one hundred and seventy years ago, is at last, completed and dedicated, a marvelous monument to the Saints of Far West. Such a sacred structure would radiate the theme, *"Holiness to the Lord, The House of the Lord"* and gloriously fulfill the hopes, dreams, and visions of the precious Saints who once made up the city of Far West.

That sweet and sacred dream is one many share with them, including the author, who has dreamed of it since that honeymoon visit twenty-five years ago. While we do not completely know God's mind and will in that matter, the author's heart aches, and his soul yearns for a future season when he might worship in the Holy Temple at Far West.

A Coming Day

> *Oh Lord whose coming draweth nigh*
> *Whose Saints still face both trial and test*
> *Wilt thou not hear, Thy servant's cry*
> *And build Thy temple at Far West?*
>
> *Thy houses stand at old Nauvoo;*
> *On Winter Quarter's holy hill.*
> *Thy Kirtland home remains to view*
> *Yet Far West's lot is empty still*
>
> *Remember Lord, that blessed time*
> *When cornerstones with joy were laid*
> *Hosanna shouts toward heaven did climb*
> *And Saints implored for heaven's aid*

Saints' souls are gone, their days long past
Consistent with Thy holy plan
Yet will Thou not, at long, long last
Let us build where, they once began

Though weak, unworthy, as I live
I ache to see that temple stand
What e'r Thou ask, dear Lord I'll give
To see Thy house, on Zion's land.

So much has changed in the years since Far West was born. The mobs have gone, or at least mellowed out and changed their tactics, and many noble, good, moral, and friendly people live in those counties where once such persecution reigned. The extermination order was repealed in 1976,[146] and a new temple has been built in the northern part of Kansas City, Missouri, just fifty or so miles south of Far West.[147] Almost nothing is the same as it was in those trying times of the 1830s, yet the sacrifices of the Far West Saints truly have sanctified that land. Their stories can be felt deep in the souls of any who take the time to visit, ponder and listen. Indeed, it is the author's hope that the essence of their sentiments, the deep meaning in their lives and their labors, have been accurately captured in this book, and adequately revealed to others through these "Whisperings from Far West."

Appendix A

Limericks of Life in Far West

1. Early on before any Saints had settled on the Shoal Creek in the region of Far West, W.W. Phelps had visited the area and written a letter from Liberty to the Prophet Joseph, in which he described his impression of what he termed the Far West. He wrote in part:

> "On Shoal creek, where there is water, there are some tolerable mill sites; but the prairies- those 'old clearings', peering one over another as far as the eye can glance, flatten all common calculations as to timber for boards, rails or future wants, for a thick population, according to the natural reasoning of man.
>
> What the design of our heavenly Father was, or is, as to these vast prairies of the Far West, I know no further than we have revelation. The Book of Mormon terms them, the land of desolation; and when I get into a prairie so large that I am out of sight of timber, just as a seaman is "out of sight of land on the oceans" I have to exclaim- 'what are man and his works compared with the Almighty and His Creations? Who hath viewed His everlasting fields?' ..."[148]

When the Saints, first looked on, Far West prairie
What they saw seemed so vast and so scary
Yet with faith in their God
Each Saint busted the sod
In rich earth, seeds of faith, they did bury

2. As mentioned previously the Lord gave a short but very meaningful revelation to the faithful and dedicated Brigham Young, which spoke powerfully of the Lord's concern for Brigham's children and wife.

"Brother Brigham," said the Lord, at Far West
"In this great work you have never sought rest"
"To my counsel give heed"
"For your family's in need"
"Care for them now, that their lives, may be blest"

3. Where the true and restored Gospel is in flower there have also been false and lying spirits that would press upon and tempt the Saints. From the beginning of the Church with Hiram Page's seer stone even up to today, there are those who are led from the truth by false revelations and lying spirits. It was no different at Far West. In a very interesting almost humorous Church disciplinary council, the recorded minutes from Far West mention a brother Lyon who was brought before the council for making false claims to a married woman in order to secure her hand in marriage. The minutes record:

> ...He claimed to have had a revelation that a Sister Jackson, who was a married woman, and whose husband was still living, was to become his wife. Lyon claimed that it had been revealed to him that the woman's husband was dead. He exerted undue influence in persuading her of these things, and she consented to be his wife; but before they were married the woman's husband appeared on the scene, *with the result, of course, that the perspective marriage did not take place.*[149]

Brother Lyon to the Sister while lying
Claimed the Lord to his soul had been crying
That her husband was dead
And 'twas him she should wed
When her husband showed up, he quit trying.

4. Among the Saints there were those who had tried to set up shops that would sell liquor to the Saints. It was at Far West where the Church had strongly re-emphasized the importance of living the Word of Wisdom, and in order to assist the Saints, the First Presidency, High Council, and Bishop's Court assembled at

Far West on 26 July 1838, added to their list of other resolutions regarding the Church, resolution Sixth, which stated:

> That we use our influence to put a stop to the selling of liquors in the city of Far West, or in our midst, that our streets may not be filled with drunkenness; and that we use our influence to bring down the price of provisions.[150]

Some merchants to make money quicker
At Far West, tried to sell the Saints liquor
But the Prophet said no
To such places we'll not go
So the business was gone in a flicker

5. As previously mentioned, on April 26, 1839, at the conclusion of the great fulfillment of the Lord's command for the Twelve to leave for their missions from the temple lot in Far West, Brother Turley, who was present at the meeting held on that sacred spot of ground, had a remarkable experience. While proceeding on with Heber C. Kimball, he expressed a desire to stop for a moment at the home of one of the brethren who had apostatized from the Church, and whose apostasy was based in part upon the seeming impossibility of the revelation being fulfilled. The home Brother Turley wanted to stop at, was that of Isaac Russell, and Brother Turley only wanted to stop long enough to show him that the prophecy was not in vain. Church History records:

> As the Saints were passing away from the meeting, Brother Turley said to Elders Page and Woodruff, "Stop a bit while I bid Isaac Russell good bye;" and knocking at the door called Brother Russell. His wife answered "Come in, it is Brother Turley." Russell replied, "It is not, he left here two weeks ago" and appeared quite alarmed; but on finding it was Brother Turley, asked him to sit down; but the latter replied, "I cannot I shall lose my company." "who is your company?" enquired Russell. "The Twelve"... "*The Twelve*"... Yes, don't you know that this is the twenty-sixth, and the day the Twelve were to take leave of their friends on the foundation of the Lord's house, to go to the Islands

of the sea? The revelation is now fulfilled, and I am going with them." Russell was speechless, and Turley bid him farewell.[151]

An apostate named Russell, quite surely
Was surprised by the visit from Turley
Prophecy he had mocked
Now fulfilled left him shocked
The Twelve met at Far West that day, early

Appendix B

Revocation of the Extermination Order

In 1976, Missouri Governor Christopher Bond rescinded Executive Order 44 as follows:

> WHEREAS, on October 27, 1838, the Governor of the State of Missouri, Lilburn W. Boggs, signed an order calling for the extermination or expulsion of Mormons from the State of Missouri; and
>
> WHEREAS, Governor Boggs' order clearly contravened the rights to life, liberty, property and religious freedom as guaranteed by the Constitution of the United States, as well as the Constitution of the State of Missouri; and
>
> WHEREAS, in this bicentennial year as we reflect on our nation's heritage, the exercise of religious freedom is without question one of the basic tenets of our free democratic republic;
>
> Now, THEREFORE, I, CHRISTOPHER S. BOND, Governor of the State of Missouri, by virtue of the authority vested in me by the Constitution and the laws of the State of Missouri, do hereby order as follows:
>
> Expressing on behalf of all Missourians our deep regret for the injustice and undue suffering which was caused by the 1838 order, I hereby rescind Executive Order Number 44, dated October 27, 1838, issued by Governor W. Boggs.
>
> In witness I have hereunto set my hand and caused to be affixed the great seal of the State of Missouri, in the city of Jefferson, on this 25 day of June, 1976.
>
> (Signed) Christopher S. Bond, Governor.[152]

END NOTES

[1] History of the Church, (HC) Volume 3, Pages 4-8.
[2] Doctrine and Covenants (D & C) 105:2-6, 9.
[3] HC, Volume 2, Page 466
[4] Doctrine and Covenants (D & C) 105:9 & 13.
[5] Luke 12:19 King James Version (KJV)
[6] HC, Volume 2, Page 468
[7] Jonah 4:7 King James Version (KJV)
[8] Doctrine and Covenants (D & C) 105:6
[9] HC, Volume 5, Page 137
[10] Jonah 4:10 King James Version (KJV)
[11] HC, Volume 2, Page 496
[12] Ibid. Page 508, emphasis added
[13] D & C 115:7
[14] HC, Volume 2, Page 483
[15] Ibid, Page 496
[16] Ibid. Page 505
[17] Ibid Page 521.
[18] D & C Section 115: 8-16
[19] HC, Volume 3, Pages 41-42.
[20] D & C 101: 2 & 6
[21] 3 Nephi 6:13
[22] Proverbs 16:18
[23] http://www.mormonwiki.com/Lyman_Wight
[24] H C Volume 2, Page 481
[25] Ibid.
[26] H C Volume 2, page 511.
[27] H C Volume 3, Page 16
[28] Ibid. Page 18
[29] HC, volume 3, pages 18-19.
[30] Ibid. Page 19
[31] HC, Volume 4, Page 142
[32] Ibid. Page 167
[33] Ibid. Page 168
[34] HC, Volume 2, Page; http://www.saintswithouthalos.com/m/380413.phtml
[35] HC, Volume 4, Page 389
[36] http://en.wikipedia.org/wiki/Lyman_E._Johnson
[37] HC, Volume 1. Page 323
[38] HC, Volume 3. page 46.
[39] HC, Volume 4. Page 69.

[40] Ibid. Page 110.
[41] HC, Volume 2, pages 187-189
[42] Ibid. Pages 333-337.
[43] HC, Volume 3 pages 165-169.
[44] Ibid. Page 345.
[45] Ibid. page 379
[46] HC, Volume 4 Page 2.
[47] HC, Volume 2, page 194
[48] Ibid. Pages 219-220
[49] Ibid. Page 491
[50] D & C Section 112.
[51] HC, Volume 2 Pages 522-527
[52] HC, Volume 3, Page 28
[53] Ibid. Pages 3-9 and 165-167.
[54] Ibid. Page 284.
[55] Journal of Discourses, 5:206.
[56] HC, Volume 2, Pages 494 & 508.
[57] HC, Volume 3, Pages 226, 339-343.
[58] Ibid Page 343-344.
[59] Ibid. Page 336
[60] http://books.google.com/books?id=fNkBAAAAMAAJ&pg=RA1-PA47&lpg=RA1-PA47&dq=%22Isaac+Russell%22+wife+Salt+Lake&source=web&ots=PmxuVGhA1E&sig=ttdcZOG8mceSpGiJGLigo5OSvgM&hl=en&sa=X&oi=book_result&resnum=5&ct=result
[61] HC, Volume 2, Page 529
[62] HC, Volume 3, Page 261
[63] HC, Volume 1, Page 323,324 emphasis added
[64] HC, Volume 3. Page 178
[65] HC, Volume 3, Pages 178-182
[66] Ibid.
[67] Ibid. Page 168 notes
[68] HC, Volume 3, Pages 8-9.
[69] Ibid. Page 12.
[70] While the word Aristarchy does not appear in modern dictionaries, in Webster's 1828 dictionary the word did exist and gave the definition as; "A body of good men in power, or government by excellent men." See: http://1828.sorabji.com/1828/words/a/aristarchy.html
[71] While the meter and form may seem strange, those who know of Chaismas and Isaiah, will understand this form.
[72] In my yet to be published book *Anatomy of the Anti-Mormon*, I detail many examples from the Bible of totally accepted and revered prophets

who declared things in the name of the Lord, which did not come to pass, based on agency and the actions of a merciful Father in Heaven. One example is Isaiah Chapter 38, KJV.

[73] D & C 138:57
[74] D & C 115: 4
[75] Abraham 3:13
[76] Revelation 2: 6, 14-15.
[77] *Doctrinal New Testament Commentary,* 3:446. @ http://www.ldsces.org/inst_manuals/dc-in/dc-in-111.htm
[78] D & C 117:12-16.
[79] http://en.wikipedia.org/wiki/William_Marks_(Latter_Day_Saints)
[80] http://en.wikipedia.org/wiki/Newel_K._Whitney
[81] http://en.wikipedia.org/wiki/Oliver_Granger
[82] HC, Volume 3, Pages 307-308.
[83] HC, Volume 3, Page 23.
[84] See D&C Section 126.
[85] HC, Volume 3, Page 46.
[86] Joseph Smith History, 1:1
[87] HC, Volume Three, page 26.
[88] JSH 1:60
[89] D & C 78: 15, 20
[90] D & C 95:17
[91] H.C. Volume 3, Page 35
[92] *Mormon Doctrine*, Bruce R. McConkie, (Book Craft: Salt Lake City) 1966 Page 21.
[93] Daniel 7:9-14
[94] History of the Church, Volume 3, page 14
[95] Ibid. Page 30
[96] Ibid. Page 51.
[97] Ibid. Page 52.
[98] Ibid. Pages 53 & 54.
[99] Ibid. Page 56
[100] Ibid. Pages 57-58
[101] Ibid. Page 59 Emphasis added
[102] HC, Volume 3 Pages 59-76
[103] Ibid. Page 68
[104] Ibid. Page 88.
[105] Ibid. Page 91.
[106] D & C 124:15
[107] HC, Volume 3, Page 99.
[108] Ibid. Page 110.
[109] Ibid. Page 137.

[110] Ibid Pages 149-162
[111] Ibid Page 158-159.
[112] Ibid Page 163
[113] http://saintswithouthalos.com/p/1838_pers_hyrum.phtml
[114] Ibid Page 163.
[115] Ibid. Pages 163-170.
[116] Ibid. Pages 171-172
[117] Ibid. Page 170
[118] http://en.wikipedia.org/wiki/David_W._Patten
[119] , Ibid. See Also: http://saintswithouthalos.com/b/patten_dwh.phtml
[120] D & C Section 124, verses 19, 130
[121] http://saintswithouthalos.com/b/patten_dwh.phtml
[122] Ibid.
[123] H of C Volume 3, Page 175.
[124] Ibid. Page 171
[125] Ibid page 175
[126] Ibid. Pages 183-187, 323,326
[127] Ibid. Page 190
[128] D & C Section 122:6
[129] H of C Volume 3, Page 193.
[130] Ibid Page 447
[131] D & C Section 121:1
[132] HC, Volume 3, page 203.
[133] Ibid. Pages 224-225
[134] Ibid. Pages 226-227
[135] Ibid. Pages 226-233.
[136] Ibid. Page 251
[137] Ibid pages 264-265
[138] Ibid. Pages 274-275
[139] Ibid. Pages 315-316.
[140] Ibid pages 321-322
[141] http://www.jwha.info/mmff/viator.htm
[142] H of C Volume 3, Page 326
[143] http://www.jwha.info/mmff/viator.htm
[144] http://www.solomonspalding.com/docs/eldjur03.htm The author of the poem is not listed but the story of the death of James Marsh and his remarkable visions is contained within the pages of the Elder's Journal.
[145] http://www.farwesthistory.com/stevens.asp
[146] For a copy of the repeal see Appendix B.
[147] The Kanas City Missouri Temple was dedicated May 6, 2012.
[148] HC Volume 2. Page 445
[149] HC, Volume 3, Page 26 emphasis added

[150] HC, Volume 3, Page 48
[151] HC, Volume 3, Pages 339-340
[152] http://www.quaqua.org/extermination.htm

Made in the USA
Columbia, SC
29 September 2024